Using Computers
in History

Using Computers in History

Sonja Cameron and Sarah Richardson

First published 2005 by
PALGRAVE MACMILLAN
Houndmills, Basingstoke, Hampshire RG21 6XS and
175 Fifth Avenue, New York, N.Y. 10010
Companies and representatives throughout the world

PALGRAVE MACMILLAN is the global academic imprint of the Palgrave Macmillan division of St. Martin's Press, LLC and of Palgrave Macmillan Ltd. Macmillan® is a registered trademark in the United States, United Kingdom and other countries. Palgrave is a registered trademark in the European Union and other countries.

ISBN-13: 978–1–4039–3415–4 hardback
ISBN-10: 1–4039–3415–0 hardback
ISBN-13: 978–1–4039–3416–1 paperback
ISBN-10: 1–4039–3416–9 paperback

This book is printed on paper suitable for recycling and made from fully managed and sustained forest sources.

A catalogue record for this book is available from the British Library.

A catalog record for this book is available from the Library of Congress.

10 9 8 7 6 5 4 3 2 1
14 13 12 11 10 09 08 07 06 05

Printed in China

Contents

List of Figures

List of Tables

Acknowledgements

Using computers in historical research is often a collaborative endeavour and the research and preparation for this book confirms this. We are indebted to the assistance we have received from friends, colleagues and students in the preparation of this book for publication. In particular, we would like to thank our colleagues: Donald Spaeth at the University of Glasgow; Tim Lockley and Jonathan Davies at the University of Warwick; and Matthew Davies, Jean Morrin, Sonja Needs, Adrienne Rosen and Mike Taylor at the University of Oxford. Our undergraduate and postgraduate students at Glasgow, Oxford and Warwick have proved extremely helpful, not only in providing some of the data we use as examples in the book but also as a sounding board for the techniques we describe here.

We have attempted to include examples throughout the text drawing on a diverse range of historical sources from a variety of chronological periods and geographical areas. This we hope will encourage historians involved in many alternative types of history using very different sources to incorporate the computer as a tool for their research. A large proportion of the data was acquired from the History section of the *Arts and Humanities Data Service* [http://ahds.ac.uk/history/] and we would like to thank staff there for their assistance. In particular we would like to acknowledge the depositors of the following data sets:

- J. K. McConica, *Prosopography of Corpus Christi College, Oxford, 1517–1603* [computer file], Colchester, Essex: UK Data Archive [distributor], 30 April 1998, SN: 3789. Depositors: Bailey, S., University of Oxford, Bodleian Library, Oxford University Archives. Principal Investigator: J. K. McConica, University of Oxford, All Souls College. Sponsor: University of Oxford. Oxford University Computing Services were responsible for the technical management of the project. Copyright: Corpus Christi College (Oxford).
- B. Godfrey, *Prosecutions for Violent Offences in Selected English, Australian and New Zealand Petty Sessions' Courts, 1880–1914* [computer file], Colchester, Essex: UK Data Archive [distributor], 19 July 2002, SN: 4483. Depositor: B. Godfrey, Keele University, Department of Criminology. Principal Investigator: B. Godfrey, Keele University, Department of Criminology. Sponsor: Economic and Social Research Council Grant Number: R000223300. Copyright: B. Godfrey.

- R. S. Schofield and E. A. Wrigley, Parish Register Aggregate Analyses, 1662–1811; 404 Data [computer file], Colchester, Essex: UK Data Archive [distributor], April 2003, SN: 4491. Principal Investigators: R. S. Schofield and E. A. Wrigley, Cambridge Group for the History of Population and Social Structure. Sponsor: Social Science Research Council. Copyright: Local Population Studies.

The Harbury Census database was created by students taking the Advanced Diploma in Local History via the Internet at the University of Oxford, 2003–04. We would like to thank their tutor, Tim Lockley for permission to use this database. The Beverley Census database was created at the University of Hull and we would like to thank Peter Adman and W. A. Speck for permission to use the data. The London Compositors Database was created from the London Compositors archive deposited in the Modern Records Centre, University of Warwick, ref: MSS 28/CO/1/9/4. We would like to thank Christine Woodland, the archivist at the Modern Records Centre and the Graphical Print and Media Union for permission to reproduce and extract from the 1890 Annual Report. All other databases, spreadsheets and images were created by the authors.

We are very grateful to Donald Spaeth for allowing the authors to read his unpublished article 'Representing Text as Data: The Analysis of Historical Sources in XML', which provided an important insight into the practical use of XML databases in historical research. The data for Figure 5.9 was supplied by the Organisation for Economic Co-operation and Development and for Figure 5.13 by the Office for National Statistics. Figure 5.19 was also supplied by the Office for National Statistics and is Crown Copyright, reference: GD272361. Tess Richardson provided her expertise in improving the design of the graphs and charts in Chapter 5. Microsoft, Encarta, MSN and Windows are either registered trademarks or trademarks of Microsoft Corporation in the United States and/or other countries. All trade marks and registered names are fully acknowledged.

SONJA CAMERON
SARAH RICHARDSON

1 Introduction: Information and Communications Technology and the Historian

The computer – or more precisely information and communications technology (ICT) – is now an essential tool for the historian and historical study. Today's 'history workstation' includes computers, modems, scanners, printers, digital cameras and a paraphernalia of software packages to access resources and analyse historical source material. The computer is a central feature in libraries, archives and competes for space with books and manuscripts on the historian's desk. Even those most resistant to the lure of the machine use computer-based library catalogues and word process their books, articles, dissertations and essays. The skills required for computer-based research and writing are natural developments from the 'traditional' skills used by historians but have helped to transform the study of history over the past three decades (at least). Whereas in the early days of mainframe technology, the computer's contribution to history was viewed in terms of crude data analysis or 'number crunching', the major current use is for locating and retrieving information via the internet. However, to reduce the role of ICT either to simple quantification or merely to accessing information would be to overlook the rich and complex part the computer has to play in the work of the historian.

One factor which faces all users of ICT is the rapid obsolescence of both hardware and software. Analogies have been made with the 'new technology' of the book in fifteenth-century Europe (see the Guide to further reading at the end of this chapter). During the Renaissance, the printing revolution resulted in exponential increases in the numbers of books in circulation and this had dramatic implications for the use and spread of knowledge, and on methods of information storage and retrieval. The advent of the personal computer with windows operating systems and the internet has transformed the way in which historians organise their work. The vast expansion of digitised text databases which utilise the technology of networks, hypertexts and mark-up languages is but one example of how rapidly historians' research skills are changing in this digital world. However, these swift leaps forward also bring problems to the researcher. Data tied to one particular piece of software may be irretrievable if the programme is not updated for use with new versions of operating systems. The integrity and quality of some information may also be suspect. Websites frequently appear and disappear and keeping track of information is often difficult. Historians therefore need to develop strategies to cope with the brisk pace of technological change. These could include considering strategies to keep up to date with resources on websites by regularly checking key library and information sites or producing copies of data in standard formats such as ASCII so that they are readily importable into a variety of software platforms.

ICT skills are widely recognised as an essential component of any undergraduate degree in History. In the United Kingdom, for example, these were specified by the Quality Assurance Agency for Higher Education (QAA) which encouraged students 'to make imaginative use of the library, the Web etc. to expand their knowledge base and their range of historical approaches'. For all History undergraduates ICT provides skills in asking questions about historical data, in the statistical and graphical analysis of sources and for bibliographic and archival searching. These skills now rely heavily upon the use of ICT yet are consistent with the pre-computer aims and objectives of historical study. ICT skills are also fundamental tools for post-graduate study and have now infiltrated all aspects of historical study. ICT is more than merely a transferable skill acquired incidentally through the study of history which will serve graduates' needs in the employment market. It is an integral part of historical study and supports all stages of historical enquiry.

This book will provide an essential introduction to all those engaged in historical study and research:

- Undergraduate students
- Graduate/postgraduate students
- Local and family historians
- History professionals.

For undergraduate and postgraduate historians the book will aid in the acquisition or enhancement of ICT skills and enable them both to produce historical work of good quality and to satisfy the requirements of funding and accreditation bodies. It will also support and enhance the use of ICT for historical study in the widest possible sense. For one of the major benefits of ICT is that it has brought the wider historical community together. Research into particular methodologies appropriate to computer-based study, the development of software or specialised tools for the analysis of historical sources, and the digitisation of historical texts and manuscripts have been undertaken by local and family historians, archivists, museum curators, librarians and enthusiasts, as well as by 'professional' historians. The internet has allowed the dissemination and exchange of information and material to become far more extensive and the digitisation of major collections has widened access beyond the traditional scholarly community. The genealogist researching a family tree and the local historian compiling a community database of historical sources require recourse to the computer as much as the undergraduate history student or professional researcher.

This book seeks to fulfil the needs of all these users and recognises that all those engaged in historical research and study have similar basic requirements:

- To locate, retrieve and manage a wide variety of material, ranging from biblio-graphic matter to primary sources;
- To interrogate and analyse critically the material gathered; and
- To prepare, write and present high quality pieces of writing.

All of these areas are covered here and the book is presented as a practical guide to assist in the research and writing of historical work. No prior knowledge of computing is assumed, and with the exception of Chapter 2 no particular software packages are used. Instead, the basic facilities and functions applicable to the leading software programs are discussed. Step-by-step instructions are given so that the readers may construct their project or undertake their research from scratch. Where appropriate, suggestions for further and/or advanced study are given at the ends of chapters.

Chapter 2 discusses presentation matters ranging from the basic requirements to word process a piece of historical writing to more complex uses of word processing packages to assist longer compositions or dissertations. Particular attention is given to the production of a piece of work which will conform to the scholarly protocols required for examination or publication. The chapter ends with a guide to creating presentations using Microsoft PowerPoint in recognition that much dissemination of historical research now takes this format rather than more formal paper-based productions.

The exponential growth of the World Wide Web is perhaps the major innovation of the last decade. Chapter 3 explores its use for historical research and as a biblio-graphic tool. The different tools for searching the Web are examined and evaluated including directories, portals and search engines. There is a review of particular sig-nificant resources for historians using the Web focusing on archives, collections of digital sources and abstracts from historical and humanities literature. The chapter is also focused on the essential area of evaluating information located on the Web and provides practical tips to ensure the authenticity and authority of individual websites and resources.

Chapter 4 introduces the creation and analysis of a database from historical sources. The chapter details the different forms of databases from flat-file or single table examples to the more complex relational models and gives examples of these databases based on a range of historical source material. The processes of database creation are discussed stage-by-stage including: planning the project; analysing the data; designing and creating the database; tips for efficient data entry; and providing clear supporting documentation for the database. The various ways to interrogate, analyse and retrieve information from an historical data set are discussed and the chapter provides a brief overview of some of the methodological approaches that historians have employed when investigating particular historical sources. The chapter ends with an outline of some of the recent developments in database technology including utilising Extensible Mark-up Language (XML) to analyse historical data and the creation of online databases.

Chapter 5 considers the three main uses of spreadsheets as a tool for historical analysis: to perform calculations and statistical operations; to act as a simple database; and to present information in a table, graph or chart. Although the chapter does not pretend to offer a full guide to the use of quantitative methods with historical sources, there is an outline of the main statistical tools used by historians. The section on the spreadsheet's use as a simple database will encourage those who want a software package to perform multiple tasks: including to undertake basic analyses of historical datasets without resorting to a relational database program. The drawbacks of using spreadsheets for data analysis as well as the opportunities offered are discussed. To complement the focus on presentation in Chapter 2, there is a full discussion of the appropriate use of graphs and charts to display historical data. There are examples of a wide range of different graphs and charts with tips on how to select the most suitable chart for specific types of historical information. The chapter ends with a discussion of complex statistical analysis software for readers requiring more sophisticated tools to interrogate their data.

In recognition that today's computing historian is concerned as much with text analysis as with numbers, Chapter 6 surveys the use of digital texts and images in historical research. The relative ease of digitising text and images has led to a mass of information becoming available to the historian via libraries, archives or publishers. The chapter investigates basic computer-aided text analysis using a straightforward package whilst signposting more advanced packages, and the use of XML for those wanting more advanced analytical tools. The use of digital images are then examined and the chapter gives an overview of the creation, access and manipulation of images for use by historians. The chapter ends with some hints and tips for creating Web pages.

Finally, there is a comprehensive glossary for readers who require full definitions for some of the technical terms used in the book, although we try to ensure that explanations of specialised language are also provided in the text. There is also a list of books and articles for further reading to supplement the information given in the book.

▶ The historian's workstation

There are a wide variety of machines available on the market. The first decision that needs to be made is whether to purchase a desktop computer or to select a portable solution such as a notebook, laptop or palm top machine. The latter have the advantage of being flexible. They may be taken to libraries and archives as well as being used at home for writing and research. Note that most libraries now insist that laptops have a certificate of electrical safety before they will allow them to be plugged into their electrical supply. The principal disadvantage of laptops is that their portable nature means that the keyboards and monitors are often more cramped and fiddly to use than those supplied with desktops. Prolonged periods of intensive writing on laptop computers should probably be avoided. Palm top computers are frequently used in conjunction with desktops. They are usually no larger than the size of a standard paperback and run 'mini' versions of the main software applications. Once back home, the information collected is easily downloaded onto a desktop computer for further analysis.

A computer that has the capability to be connected to the internet is probably the minimum requirement for the historian's workstation. However, the purchase of further equipment will enhance the opportunities available for historical research. This equipment might include: printers, scanners and digital cameras. Most ink-based printers will now normally produce colour as well as black and white copies. This facility allows for the production of high quality pictures, photographs and graphs, either on paper or as slides. Laser printers produce high quality copies which may be used as camera ready copy for desktop publishing. Scanners allow both text and images to be captured as digital images. Once digitised, they may be enhanced for ease of use or legibility or, in the case of text, be translated into a machine-readable form. Digital cameras are becoming a common tool for the historian. Many archives and libraries will permit the use of digital cameras to copy material as they are less harmful to manuscripts and texts than the photocopier. Equipment to back-up data or to store large picture, sound or movie files are also essential. Current technology is advancing rapidly and most users now employ flash drives which connect to a computer's USB port, re-writeable CD-ROMs, or DVDs, rather than the older zip disks or floppy disks.

The capturing of images and copying of material confronts the historian with certain ethical issues, particularly copyright, data protection and freedom of information. Many organisations publish guidance on good research practice (see Guide to Further Reading at the end of the chapter). These guidelines usually incorporate principles of integrity, openness, responsibility, good practice and ethical conduct.

Copyright material may be text, images, computer programs, recordings or films. Copyright does not protect ideas but the way the idea is expressed. Copyright offers protection regardless of the medium and therefore material published on the internet is subject to the same restraints. In some countries fair dealing rules permit the use of copyrighted material for personal research purposes but do not allow the copying or transmission of that information to a third party either in the form of a paper copy or electronically. Therefore images or text digitised for personal use may be permitted but if the information is published in any form, including on a website, then full written permission must be obtained from the copyright holder(s). Copyright law differs from place to place, for example the European Union and the United States have differing regulations, so users should check carefully the current legal situation in their own country. Many archives have more restrictive clauses for use of manuscripts in their possession. Most uses of copyright material require permission from the copyright owner. When in any doubt over copyright issues check with the copyright owner and give full details of intended use.

Data Protection and Freedom of Information legislation usually applies to any living individual which has implications for those working on contemporary records. Researchers are responsible for ensuring that data on individuals is not used in a way that could cause substantial distress and damage, and that results are not made available in a form that could identify any individual. Therefore anonymised information, such as a case study, may be published but no individual should be named without their consent. Ethical good practice also requires confidentiality. Again, regulations differ from country to country so check that work conforms to local regulations.

The key software applications for the historian include: an internet browser, word processing software, a spreadsheet package and a relational database management system. Though not essential, further programs which allow the manipulation of digital images, optical character readers, Web publishers, bibliographic software, text analysis programs and statistical packages, may be desirable for historians with particular needs. There are many alternative software suites and programs available on the market and it is advisable to have experience of more than one program before making a purchase. If possible, try out programs using historical data and draw up a list of essential requirements so that a full assessment of the software may be undertaken.

Modern computing practices inevitably imply an interaction with other machines and users. This book outlines the many benefits that this communication will have for historians. However, linking your computer with others is also a hazardous pursuit. Therefore, computer 'safety' should be of paramount concern for anyone using computers and exchanging information with others. There are five main ways in which personal computers may be protected:

Anti-virus and spyware software

A **virus** is a programme that infiltrates a computer usually by clandestine methods. Once resident on the host computer it is capable of replicating itself with little or no user intervention. Viruses may be benign but are often malicious and may alter or delete files or transmit information from the host computer to others. They are often disguised as games or encourage users to open files with innocuous titles such as 'Memo' or 'Xmas pictures'. A **worm** is a virus that spreads by creating duplicates of itself on other drives, systems or networks. Worms may send copies of themselves to other computers via network connections or e-mail. Increasingly worms are exploiting internet messaging software. Some programmes that infect computers do not replicate themselves. These are often called **Trojans** and are not technically viruses. The programme presents itself as having a set of useful or desirable features but in reality contains material that may damage the host computer. Often Trojans are used by viruses and worms to infiltrate a computer initially. Viruses spread by using e-mails, bulletin boards and networks. Users may also spread viruses by sending contaminated files by e-mail or on a disk to other users. Therefore it is important not to open any files attached to e-mails if they come from an unknown source. Even if the source is known and trustworthy be sure that you know what an attachment is before you open it. Check any downloaded files with anti-virus software before opening them. Anti-virus software should be installed on all computers but it needs to be regularly updated. As many as 500 new viruses are uncovered each month so anti-virus software quickly goes out of date. Most companies offering anti-virus products allow regular and automatic updating of their software. Most users are now sensitive to the problem of viruses. Some high profile cases where companies have been targeted by viruses has increased awareness of the problem. However, of equal inconvenience is the issue of virus hoaxes. Virus hoaxes may lead users into deleting genuine files, or filling up e-mail inboxes warning others of potential viruses, or encouraging them to ignore all virus warning messages assuming that they are hoaxes too.

A related issue is the increasing amount of junk e-mail or **spam** that fills up e-mail inboxes. These e-mail messages are not viruses but have a similar effect on users by obscuring genuine e-mails and taking up space on hard drives and servers. Many e-mail programmes now have filters or spam-controls to block such messages but these may also stop genuine messages from getting through.

A recent variation of viruses is **spyware**. Spyware is software that collects personal information from computers without the user's knowledge or permission. This may include usernames and passwords. Spyware is able to track sites the computer has visited on the internet, to send this information to a third party, to change browser home pages and add toolbars, to alter system files and to install pop-up windows. Signs that spyware has been installed on a computer are: Internet connection speeds are slower; unwanted pop-up adverts appear sometimes even when the computer is not attached to the internet; Web browser settings or home pages change and keep reverting to a particular site; the computer is slow and unresponsive. There is free spyware detection software available and many anti-virus packages are now including spyware detection as part of their services.

Update operating systems regularly

Microsoft and Apple Macintosh regularly update their operating systems in order to safeguard against security issues in their software. A personal computer may be set to download and update the operating system regularly. This protects personal machines against hackers and may safeguard them against some viruses.

Install firewalls

A **firewall** is a piece of software or hardware that filters communications between a computer or network and the internet. A firewall protects a computer from unauthorised access by monitoring incoming traffic from a network and only allowing connections that have been explicitly permitted.

Back-up files regularly

All computers are susceptible to various types of failure and therefore having regular routines to back-up files is essential. Power cuts, physical failures of hard disk drives, software crashes, virus attacks and errors by users could all mean that vital data is lost and is irrecoverable. At the very least, documents created by you which cannot be easily replaced should be regularly backed-up. These files should also be saved frequently in case of sudden computer failure. The frequency of back-ups depends on the amount of computer use. In periods where many new documents are being created, a daily back-up routine should be used. If there are times when computers are only used occasionally a weekly back-up schedule should be adopted. The most straightforward method of backing up files is to copy all the required documents to a back-up medium. Suitable media for backing up files include networks, flash memory sticks, writeable or re-writable CDs, zip drives and external hard drives. Floppy disks which typically have a capacity of only 1.44 MB are becoming obsolete and many personal computers are no longer supplied with drives to read the disks. However, there are also software packages which will allow more sophisticated back-up routines and offer further services. Current operating systems also allow computer settings to be restored to an earlier date. This tool is particularly useful if a piece of software has been installed on the computer and has changed or disrupted its settings or performance. System restoration allows the computer to revert to an earlier version without deleting current document files, e-mails or changing settings in browsers.

Use passwords

One of the most common devices used to protect machines or internet accounts is the password. However if passwords are shared with others or 'cracked' by hackers then malicious users have the potential to do a wide range of damage. This may include reading or deleting important documents, accessing personal details, or launching attacks on other users and machines. There are basic precautions to protect passwords. For example passwords should not be shared with other users, they should not be written down or stored in a programme or document and they should be changed regularly. Passwords should be long and not easy to guess but they should also be easy to remember. One method is to use a mixture of upper and lower case letters, numbers and punctuation.

Working on computers for long periods may cause discomfort and possibly lead to health problems, so ensure that the workspace is designed to eliminate risks and be as comfortable as possible:

- The chair and screen should be adjusted to find the most comfortable position for work. As a guide, forearms should be horizontal and eyes should be the same height as the top of the monitor. A footrest may be helpful.
- Consider using a document holder if you will be taking notes or transcribing material. At the very least, ensure there is enough space around the machine for documents and equipment.
- Avoid glare or bright reflections on the screen. Adjust the brightness and contrast controls to suit the lighting conditions in the room. Ensure that the screen is clean and does not flicker.
- Consider using an ergonomic keyboard (i.e. one with a rest for hands and wrists in front of the keyboard). Develop a good keyboard technique that does not put too much stress on fingers.
- Do not sit in the same position for long periods. Change posture as often as is practical. Frequent short breaks from the screen and keyboard are desirable.

This book aims to support the 'training' needs of the broad historical community, from those in the formal academic system to those encountering historical research for the first time through family or local history projects; and to encourage all forms of historical endeavour. The almost unnoticed benefit of the ICT revolution has been to bring the disparate parts of that community together and improve the quality of historical research by spreading knowledge and best practice beyond the bounds of academia. In return, some of the most innovative applications of technology to historical source material has taken place outside the realm of the professional historian. This synergy of interests and enthusiasms will doubtless continue to be facilitated by technology, and we hope, in a small way, that this guide will contribute to and encourage these developments.

▶ Guide to further reading

Benjamin, Jules R., *A Student's Guide to History*, ninth edn (Boston and New York, 2004).

The Office of Research Integrity (USA): http://www.ori.hhs.gov.

Rhodes, Neil and Sawday, Jonathan, *The Renaissance Computer: Knowledge Technology in the First Age of Print* (London, 2000).

The Wellcome Trust (UK), *Guidelines on Good Research Practice*: http://www.wellcome.ac.uk.

2 A Guide to Presentation for Historians

This chapter is focused on all aspects of presenting material from a simple word processed report to a dissertation or article for publication. The software used throughout the chapter is Microsoft Word® and Microsoft Powerpoint® which are part of the Microsoft Office® suite. The chapter is divided into two sections, and here is where you decide what you need:

If all you want to do is write a presentable, academic essay, you will just need the **Basic presentation** section. We assume that you know the basics about creating and saving documents and formatting simple paragraphs, and will simply focus on the elements which are not required in an ordinary text document.

If, however, you are about to write a dissertation, or any lengthy piece of work – anything with more than a chapter, essentially – you may be better served by reading, at least, the section about **Styles** in the **Complex presentation guide** before embarking on anything else.

▶ Basic presentation guide

Presentation is important. An article essay or dissertation that is well written and properly laid out will gain your readers' confidence and convey your message to them as efficiently as possible. Above all the piece of work should be consistent in all its elements.

This section introduces the following elements which are essential in any piece of historical writing:

- Page numbers
- Headers and footers
- Footnotes and Endnotes
- Quotations
- Bibliography
- Spell checking and grammar checking.

▶ Page numbers

Page numbers are essential. You should always include them. Some Word **templates** are set to produce them automatically, but it is still good to know how to create your own, or manipulate the **default** ones you are given by the program.

How to insert page numbers

The basic way

There is a very simple way of inserting a page number into your document. Click Insert>Page Numbers, and the following dialogue box pops up (see Figure 2.1).

This screen capture shows the default. If you want your page number to appear in the middle of the top of the page, simply use the drop-down boxes to change the settings. Click OK. You now have page numbers.

The more sophisticated way

To understand how page numbers work, you have to understand about **headers** and **footers**. Every document automatically has some space assigned at the top and bottom which is meant to hold information such as page numbers, document or chapter title, author name, date of last printout, or, in fact, anything else you desire. You can see (and change) how this space is allocated by clicking File>Page Setup.

In Figure 2.2 you see that the Header and the Footer are set to 1.5 cm from the edge of the page – this means that any text or figures you insert into these fields will appear in this area.

To get to the point where you can actually insert such text and figures, cancel out what you have just done, and click View>Header and Footer instead. This will show

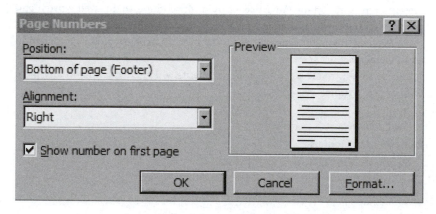

Figure 2.1　Inserting page numbers.

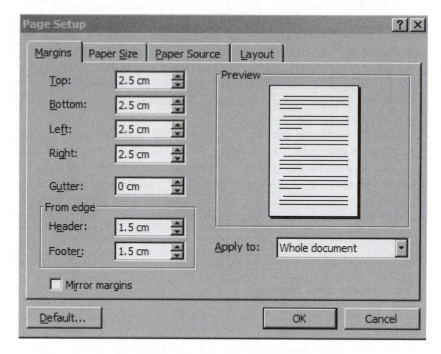

Figure 2.2   Changing the set-up of a page.

Figure 2.3   The Header and Footer toolbar.

you areas at the top and bottom of your page, bordered by a perforated-looking line. These are your header and footer fields. Believe it or not, you can simply type anything you want into these areas.

However, a little toolbar also appears (see Figure 2.3).

Right at the beginning, we recommend holding your mouse over each of the buttons on it in turn, because explanations will pop up which tell you what each button is for. Some are for inserting information; others are for switching between header and footer, or between headers/footers on different pages. It takes some getting used to, but you are intelligent and will figure it out.

To insert a page number, simply click the first button on the left while you are either in a header or a footer field. The number will appear, and by default, the count will continue on the following pages.

However, the number may not be in exactly the place you want it to be, and it may use a font you don't want, either. A useful thing to know is that although the page number is in a special **field**, you can treat it just like any ordinary piece of text in the normal part of your document. You can change font face and size by simply using the same procedure as for any other text. You can also left-align, centre, or right-align it, manipulate it with tab markers, and write text around it if you think that makes sense.

To control how the page number relates to the rest of the document, click on the third button in from the left: Format Page Number. This is not about the kind of character formatting just described in the preceding paragraph. Rather, it deals with where the number will or will not show up, and with the characters used for numbering (e.g. Arabic versus Roman). If you are using styles (see the **Complex section**), you can also set the system to recognise where a new chapter starts, and add a chapter identifier accordingly.

▶ Headers and footers

You can add anything you like to the header or footer of your page. For example, the title of your dissertation or essay, your name, or your company logo if you are setting out to be a heritage consultant. If you want to go to the trouble of setting up different headers/footers for each chapter, you can insert individual chapter titles. You can also add the complete page count to each individual page number. To take a rather fussy example, you could create a footer field that reads:

J. Doe   The Importance of Being Charles I   Page 3 of 224

How to do this? Go to your first page. Click View>Header and Footer. It will show you the first header in your document. Set your tabs so you have a centred tab in the centre of your page (to figure out where that is, hit View>Ruler if you haven't done so already) and a right-aligned tab just at the right margin.

At the start of the line, type your name (J. Doe or whatever it may be). Hit the tab key until you reach your centre tab (this may take just one hit or several, depending on your document setup). Here, type the title of your dissertation. Hit the tab key again – probably just once will be enough to get you to the right-aligned tab. Type 'Page', then click the 'Insert Page Number' on the little toolbar that came with your Header/Footer access. Type 'of', then click the 'Insert Number of Pages' button (right next to the previous one). Voila!

You may have to highlight the entire line and apply character formatting to it so it is consistent, since the automatically created numbers will probably have some default which does not correspond to the font face and size you use in the rest of the line. Luckily, you will only have to do this once.

▶ Referencing

Any historical essay or dissertation worth anything at all will have references to its sources included. These come in two forms: footnotes or endnotes for specific references, and a bibliography which lists all the material consulted in alphabetical order.

Inserting a footnote or endnote

Word makes it easy to insert footnotes or endnotes into a document. Simply click Insert>Footnote (or more quickly, type: Alt>I>N). In the dialogue box that comes up, select whether you want a footnote or an endnote (we recommend footnotes, but some publishers prefer endnotes).

Converting an endnote to a footnote and vice versa

You may have written your dissertation or essay using footnotes because after all, nobody in their right mind wants to have to flip to the back every single time they want to check a reference in your text. However, your publisher may think that footnotes clutter up the page, and insists that for tidiness if not practicality, you should place the notes at the end of the text.

The simplest way to convert all your footnotes to endnotes (and it also works the other way round) is to pretend you want to create a new foot- or endnote. So: Alt>Insert>Footnote. You will get the usual dialogue box. This time, select the Options ... button at the bottom. It will bring up a dialogue box (see Figure 2.4).

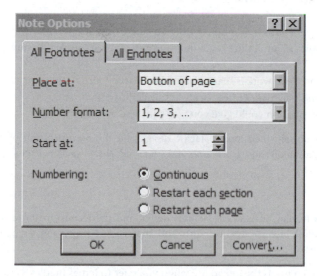

Figure 2.4   The Footnote dialogue box.

Note the Convert ... button at the bottom right. If you click on that, yet another dialogue box will appear that lets you convert between footnotes and endnotes quite easily.

Remember to delete your 'fake footnote' after this operation!

Referencing styles

A footnote or endnote number in your text should always follow quoted or cited material. They may also be used to add further information to your text, but always consider whether this extra material should appear in the main body of the work or as an appendix. Footnote or endnote reference numbers should come at the end of a sentence or at least at the end of a clause. They should *never* be placed after authors' names or other references preceding the cited matter.

There are many correct ways to format and present the references. **The most important point is to be consistent. Once you have selected a particular reference style, stick to it**. There are two main formats of referencing in scholarly works: Chicago style and Harvard style. A publisher or university will usually adopt one format or another so it is important to check which style is required before starting your piece of work. The basic elements of referencing in both styles are set out below.

Chicago style

Referencing articles

Information should appear in the following order and style:

Full name of author, 'Complete title', in single quotation marks, *Name of periodical*, in italics or underlined, volume number and part in Arabic numerals, page numbers.

The principle at work is that a book, journal (the journal itself; *not* an article in a journal) and newspaper titles are always underlined/*italicised*.

This presentation could give you two equally correct forms:

> James Bradley, 'Relational database design and the reconstruction of the British medical profession: constraints and strategies', *History and Computing*, 6: 2 (1994), 71–84.

Or

> James Bradley, 'Relational database design and the reconstruction of the British medical profession: constraints and strategies', History and Computing, 6: 2 (1994), 71–84.

This full reference is the one to use when you refer to James Bradley's article for the first time in a chapter or essay. After that initial full reference, you should use the short-form system:

> Bradley, 'Relational database design and the reconstruction of the British medical profession', p. 74.

Or

> Bradley, 'Relational database design' (1994): 74.

There is considerable confusion among writers about the meaning and status of <u>underlining</u> and *italicising*. In most referencing systems they are equivalent. In former times, before word-processors, underlining a word in handwriting or by typewriter, was the signal to a typesetter to set the word in italics. Either is correct, but once you have chosen one method, be consistent and stick to it.

Referencing single authored books

Information should appear in the following style and format:

> Full name of author, *complete Title*, <u>underlined</u>/*italicised* (place of publication, date of publication) in brackets if preferred, page number being cited. It is not necessary to show the publisher, if you do, you must be absolutely consistent in doing so throughout your text.

This format could give you several equally correct forms:

> D. I. Greenstein, <u>A Historian's guide to computing</u> (Oxford, 1994), p. 321.

Or

> D. I. Greenstein, *A Historian's guide to computing* (Oxford, 1994): 321.

Or

> D. I. Greenstein, *A Historian's guide to computing* (Oxford: Oxford University Press, 1994), p. 321.

Having decided on a format, you must use it consistently in the short-title version:

> Greenstein, <u>A Historian's guide</u> (1994): 43–54.

Or

> Greenstein, *A Historian's guide*, pp. 43–54.

Referencing multi-authored books

A similar layout applies to multi-authored books:

> Full names of authors, *complete Title*, <u>underlined</u>/*italicised* (place of publication, date of publication) in brackets if preferred, page number being cited.

E. Mawdsley and T. Munck, *Computers for historians: an introductory guide* (Manchester, 1993), pp. 333–7.

The short title would then be:

Mawdsley and Munck, *Computers for historians*, pp. 333–7.

Or

Mawdsley and Munck, <u>Computers for historians</u> (1993): 333–7.

Edited books

The same variety of formatting applies:

E. A. Wrigley, (ed.), <u>Identifying people in the past</u> (London, 1973): 33–76.

Jean-Paul Genet and A. Zampolli (eds), *Computers and the humanities* (Aldershot, 1992), pp. 63–72.

L. Burnard, 'Primary to secondary: using the computer as a tool for textual analysis in historical research', in Peter Denley and Deian Hopkin (eds), *History and Computing*, Manchester: Manchester University Press, 1987, pp. 228–33.

Charles Harvey, 'The nature and future of historical computing', in Evan Mawdsley *et al.* (eds), <u>History and Computing III: Historians, Computers and Data</u> (Manchester, 1990): 204–13.

Note that ed. is cited thus (because the full word does not end with d), but eds is cited without the full stop (because the full word does end in s)

Newspaper articles

Peter Watson, 'Stolen Art. The Unromantic Truth', *The Times*, 29 August 2003, p. 1.

This is the form to use for reference to a newspaper or a weekly magazine. No volume number is needed. It is a peculiarity of *The Times* newspaper that it registered its name with the definite article. It is always written *The Times* (or <u>The Times</u>). Other newspapers and weeklies are referred to without the definite article: *Guardian*, 21 June 2004).

Manuscripts and archives

Birmingham University Library, Court Papers, 'Court Manuscript on Coal'.

Public Record Office, HO 317/52. Letter from G. Weller to J. Armitage, 24 September 1916.

Warwickshire County Record Office, D/234, Parish of Astley, Overseers' Accounts, 1732–1741.

(All of these references to material in national and local record offices will come under the heading of 'Manuscript Sources' in your Bibliography.)

Theses

> Jane Rickard, 'James I and the illusion of magnificence: representing royalty' (PhD thesis, University of Warwick, 2003).
>
> R. E. Marshall, 'The Sheffield Mechanics Institution' (MA, Sheffield Polytechnic, 1981), p. 74.

(Note here that theses are not published, so their titles are not italicised nor underlined.)

Electronic sources

There are special conventions for citing materials from electronic media, such as online journals, databases, electronic bibliographies, World Wide Web sites, internet discussion groups and e-mail communications. The essential principles are the same as with printed works or manuscripts: sources should be acknowledged, and readers should be given the information that would allow them to check these for themselves if they wish. Formats for citation vary according to the type of medium and source material being used.

When citing a **World Wide Web** page use the following order: Author; Title of page (in quotes); title of complete work, if this page is part of a group of documents; date the page was created; URL (Internet address): http://host computer/directory path/filename; date you viewed it.

The example below demonstrates some basic principles: note that the date of creation of the work *and* the date you consulted it are both cited.

> I. Lee, 'Research, Writing, and Style Guides (MLA, APA, Chicago/Turabian, Harvard, CGOS, CBE)', 20 May 2004. http://www.aresearchguide.com/styleguides.html (26 July 2004).

Harvard style

In the Harvard system a citation in the body of the text generally requires only the name of the author(s) and the year of publication with specific pages if necessary. This appears in brackets at the end of the sentence, before the full stop. The full reference is then cited at the end of the essay or piece of work. The Harvard style replaces the need for footnotes and therefore is useful for shorter pieces of work.

Referencing articles

Harvard style is subtly different from Chicago style and is commonly used in social science periodicals and publications. For articles the details required, in order, are: name(s) of author(s) in the format: surname, and initials or given name; year of publication; title of article, in single quotation marks; title of periodical underlined or *italicised*; volume number; issue or part number; page number(s):

> Bradley, James (1992), 'Relational database design and the reconstruction of the British medical profession: constraints and strategies', *History and Computing*, 6:2, 71–84.

Or

> Bradley, J. 1992, 'Relational database design and the reconstruction of the British medical profession: constraints and strategies', <u>History and Computing</u>, vol. 6, no. 2, pp. 71–84.

Short titles are not normally used in the Harvard style. Instead, the author(s) name, date and page numbers if necessary are inserted in the text. For example: Bradley demonstrates the constraints of using a relational database to reconstruct the British medical profession (Bradley, 1992).

Single authored books

The details required for citing a single authored book are: name of author (surname, then initials or given name); year of publication; title of publication and subtitle <u>underlined</u> or *italicised*; series title and individual volume, if any; editions, if other than first, publisher, place of publication, page number(s), if applicable.

> Floud, R. 1979, *An introduction to quantitative methods for historians*, second edition London, pp. 45–67.

Multi-authored books

A similar layout applies to multi-authored books:

Full names of authors (surnames, then initials or given names); year of publication; title of publication and subtitle <u>underlined</u> or *italicised*; series title and individual volume, if any; editions, if other than first, publisher, place of publication, page number(s), if applicable.

> Mawdsley, E. and Munck, T. (1993), *Computers for historians: an introductory guide*, Manchester University Press, Manchester, pp. 333–7.

Edited books

The same variety of formatting applies:

> Wrigley, E. A. (ed.) 1973, <u>Identifying people in the past</u>, London, pp. 33–76.
>
> Burnard, L. (1987) 'Primary to secondary: using the computer as a tool for textual analysis in historical research', in <u>History and Computing</u>, eds Denley, P. and Hopkin, D., Manchester University Press, Manchester, pp. 228–33.

Newspaper articles

> Watson, Peter, 2003, 'Stolen Art. The Unromantic Truth', *The Times*, 29 August, p. 1.

Theses

Rickard, Jane, 2003, 'James I and the illusion of magnificence: representing royalty', PhD thesis, University of Warwick.

Marshall, R. E. (1981), 'The Sheffield Mechanics Institution', MA, Sheffield Polytechnic, p. 74.

Electronic sources

The basic citation is as follows: Author, surname then first names or initials; date of publication, title of publication, publisher/organisation, type of medium, date item retrieved, name or site address on internet.

Lee, I. 2004, 'Research, Writing, and Style Guides (MLA, APA, Chicago/Turabian, Harvard, CGOS, CBE)', 26 July 2004, http://www.aresearchguide.com/styleguides.html

▶ Quotations

You will have seen that in print publications, quotations longer than a line or two are usually offset from the main text, single spaced, and indented on the left (and sometimes also on the right). Of course you could click Format>Paragraph and make adjustments in the resulting dialogue box every time you have to do this, but there is a quicker way.

To indent a paragraph, hit Ctrl-M, all simultaneously. Yes, just that. To un-indent it, hit Ctrl-Shift-M.

To single-space a paragraph, hit Ctrl-1. To get $1\frac{1}{2}$ spaces, use Ctrl-5, and to double-space, Ctrl-2. Play with this. It's fun.

▶ Bibliographies

Bibliographies are usually sorted alphabetically, and have the author's last name before his or her first name.

The two main useful things to know regarding bibliographies are how to make the last names stand out a little more for easy location, and how to avoid having to do the alphabetic sorting oneself.

You may have a bibliography which consists of entries similar to these:

Davies, H. R., 'Automated record linkage of census enumerators' books and registration data. Obstacles, challenges and solutions', *History and Computing*, 4 (1992), 16–26.

Darcy, R. and Rohrs, R. C., *A guide to quantitative history* (Westport, Ct, 1995).

Denley, P., 'Models, sources and users. Historical database design in the 1990s', *History and Computing*, 6 (1994), 33–44.

This is clearly not very easy to read. One way to make it easier would be to have a blank line in between each entry. Another way is to use what is called a **Hanging indent**. This means that the first line of each entry would be flush with the left margin of the document, but the following lines of the same entry would be slightly indented. The author's name would therefore stand out from the rest, allowing the reader's eye to travel quickly down the list.

Davies, H. R., 'Automated record linkage of census enumerators' books and registration data. Obstacles, challenges and solutions', *History and Computing*, 4 (1992), 16–26.
Darcy, R. and Rohrs, R. C., *A guide to quantitative history* (Westport, Ct, 1995).
Denley, P., 'Models, sources and users. Historical database design in the 1990s', *History and Computing*, 6 (1994), 33–44.

To do this, simply highlight the paragraph or paragraphs you want to do this to, then hit Ctrl-T. (Yes, you could do it by going into Format>Paragraph and fiddling with dialogue boxes, but this is quicker.) If you have inadvertently changed a paragraph you did not want to be affected, hit Ctrl-Shift-T, and it will revert to normal.

Alphabetical order, the easy way

Word allows you to sort paragraphs alphabetically, but has hidden the function in a menu called 'Table'. This would, at first glance, seem to imply that you can only *do* this with tables, but nothing could be further from the truth!

Assume you are starting with the results of your last exercise:

Davies, H. R., 'Automated record linkage of census enumerators' books and registration data. Obstacles, challenges and solutions', *History and Computing*, 4 (1992), 16–26.
Darcy, R. and Rohrs, R. C., *A guide to quantitative history* (Westport, Ct, 1995).
Denley, P., 'Models, sources and users. Historical database design in the 1990s', *History and Computing*, 6 (1994), 33–44.

Simply highlight all of it yet again.

Now select Table>Sort (see Figure 2.5).

The defaults will probably be exactly what you need, anyway. Make sure that the 'No header row' button is selected.

OK this, and instantly, your bibliography will be alphabetised.

Darcy, R. and Rohrs, R. C., *A guide to quantitative history* (Westport, Ct, 1995).
Davies, H. R., 'Automated record linkage of census enumerators' books and registration data. Obstacles, challenges and solutions', *History and Computing*, 4 (1992), 16–26.
Denley, P., 'Models, sources and users. Historical database design in the 1990s', *History and Computing*, 6 (1994), 33–44.

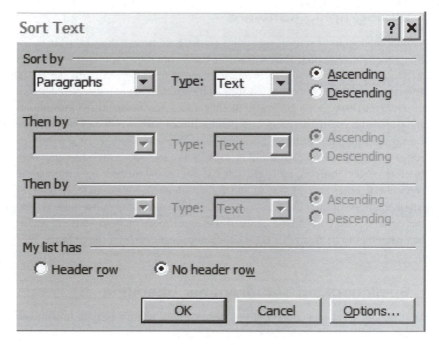

Figure 2.5 The Sort Text dialogue box.

You can do this as many times as you like, so there is no need to find the correct place to add new entries – simply put them at the bottom, and whenever you feel like it highlight the entire bibliography and go through the sorting process again.

The bibliography collects together in one place and lists all material to which reference has been made in the body of the work. **If you have not quoted from, cited, or referred to a work or a body of material in your work, then it should not be in your bibliography**.

Bibliographies are usually organised under the following subheadings:

- Manuscript sources
- Government publications
- Newspapers and periodicals
- Contemporary articles, books, pamphlets and speeches
- Published secondary sources
- Unpublished papers and theses.

▶ Bibliographic software

Bespoke bibliographic software programs are designed to take the hard work out of compiling bibliographies. They will ensure that your bibliographies and footnotes are always consistent, and will re-format them, if necessary, in particular styles. They also have the advantage of assisting in the cataloguing of bibliographies with the facility to arrange via keywords. Bibliographies may be organised into subsets and searched for particular categories. Bibliographic software is designed to manage a range of formats including monographs, journal articles, conference proceedings, edited works, theses, magazine and newspaper articles, e-mail messages and Web-based resources. However, most software packages allow the user to customise the types of references and the way in which they are cited. For example, formats for citing archives or manuscripts could be added. A further advantage is that bibliographies may be shared between users and most modern software allows bibliographies to be created in **HTML** format for publishing on the internet.

▶ Spellchecking and grammar checking

Most people use a spellchecker. If you are writing a history essay, you will very quickly have to face the fact that the spellchecker was 'Not Made For You'. It simply will not have most of the words you use, and it will suggest the oddest replacements for perfectly ordinary historical terminology.

There are two ways of dealing with this:

1. Stop using the spellchecker. Only do this if you are very confident in your spelling ability, and are prepared to proofread your document thoroughly after it is finished. Everybody makes mistakes. Everybody. Having a literate friend look over it, too, is a good idea, since by the time you are finished, you will be overly familiar with what you are saying, and worse, what you want to say. You will see words that are not there. A fresh pair of eyes will pick up things that you are simply no longer in a position to notice.
2. Train the spellchecker. The spellchecker comes with a facility that lets you add your own words to the standard dictionary, or even set up a separate dictionary to be used with particular documents.

How to train your spellchecker

After you have written perhaps ten pages, do a spell check. As soon as it comes across words like *infangandthef*, it will complain bitterly (see Figure 2.6).

At best, it will be stumped for suggestions. At worst, it will suggest some completely unrelated word for you to replace your medieval justice term with. However, looking to the right, you see three buttons.

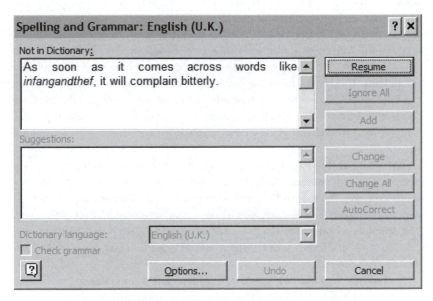

Figure 2.6   Spell checking.

'Ignore' ensures the spell checker ignores the word just this once. This can be useful if you have some outrageous spelling (something you would flag with 'sic' in the text itself) which you know will not recur, but which you also know you will never use again and do not want your computer to get used to. If you are spellcheck-ing the transcribed text of charters, for example, this would be a good option to use.

'Ignore all' causes the spell checker to ignore the word throughout the rest of the document for this particular session.

'Add', finally, makes the computer accept that, never mind what it used to believe, this is actually a genuine word. If you click the 'Add' button, the word will become included in your spell checker's dictionary, and will in future be treated as a correct spelling. Needless to say, before you do this for any given word, you should make sure it is spelt correctly.

The 'Add' function is invaluable for historians. The investment of time will be considerable at the beginning, as about every third word in your dissertation or arti-cle will require checking and adding, but after a while the system will know most of the everyday words you use, and things will speed up.

Grammar checking

Word's grammar checker will highlight sentences which it considers to be gram-matically or stylistically flawed, and it will suggest corrections. The trouble is that some of the rules it uses are not universal, some are outdated, and even those which may be perfectly appropriate to an ordinary writing environment are not appropriate in the context of academic writing. In historical writing, precision is vital, but at times precision does not make for very fluid prose. Accepting a suggestion by the grammar checker simply on the basis that 'it sounds better' or 'it is more correct' can dilute what you are actually trying to say, or (at worst) change the meaning completely. In particular, watch its treatment of commas. In academic discourse, whether (and where) you place a comma can affect the meaning of your entire sentence.

Having said all this, later versions of Word (above 97, where this function is very basic) will let you customise the grammar checker to a great extent. To do this, click Tools>Options, find the 'Spelling & Grammar' tab, and then click on 'Settings ...'. Right at the top of the dialog box, you will see a drop-down list of ready-set options. The default is probably 'Standard'. For historical writing, set it to 'Technical'. You can also scroll down the list of Grammar and Style features and select which ones it will or will not check.

On the whole, however, we urge caution with regard to the grammar checker and would suggest avoiding its use. If you are so unsure of yourself that you would feel safer using it, we recommend reading an entertaining introduction to grammar instead. They do exist, and will be of greater use to you.

▶ Complex presentation guide

This section is called complex for a reason, and the reason is the first part: Styles.

Word has a wonderful, immensely time-saving facility. Unfortunately, it is fairly complicated to grasp, and takes some effort to get it right at the beginning. Believe us, though, it's worth it.

▶ Styles

What is a Style?

Imagine you are typing a long quotation into your document. You will probably want to offset it somehow. Maybe you'll give it a 2 cm indent on either side. If your main document is double-spaced, you'll also probably want to single-space it. This is called a '**Block quotation**', and it's the accepted way of presenting quotations longer than two lines in academic publications (see also page 21). Finally, you may want to leave a wider space before and after the quotation, to offset it nicely from the text around it.

To do this, you would normally go into Format>Paragraph, and choose the appropriate settings for line spacing, left and right indent, and spaces before and after. Or you would use paragraph spacing combined with keyboard shortcuts like Ctrl-M, as described on page 21. This is simple enough.

But picture that you have a dozen of these block quotations, and have to do it for every single one of them. Then imagine that you can't quite remember – did you leave 4 points of space last time or 6 points? And suppose that you decide the default indent of 2 cm is too much after all, and you want to change them all to 1.5 cm. All 54 of them.

There is a better way. Word allows you to make the changes once and give the resulting paragraph format – the 'style' – a name. Next time you want to make the same changes, you simply select the name from a drop down list, and your paragraph will obediently assume the required shape.

In addition, if you want to make overall changes, all you need to change is the style, and all the paragraphs which are based on that style will change automatically.

If you are going to create a sizeable piece of work, do spend some time setting up your styles first of all. It may take you a couple of hours (yes, hours), but it will save you a lot of hassle in the long run, and you will have a very professional and consistent looking document at the end. Moreover, once you have your styles set up, you can re-use them for future documents of a similar type.

Finding styles

The styles you are most likely to need are the following:

- Normal
- Heading 1
- Heading 2 (and so on depending on how many sub-levels or chapters your work is going to have)
- Footnote marker
- Footnote paragraph
- Block quotation
- Bibliography.

All except the last two should be called exactly that. The reason for this is that these styles are already predefined by Word (though perhaps not quite the way you want them to look) and are used by default for various automatic functions. We will get to that later.

Have a look at your formatting toolbar after you have just opened a document. Normally, it has a drop-down box at the far left, and within that box, the text will probably read 'Normal' (see Figure 2.7).

Figure 2.7 The toolbar showing the current style.

If it does not, you are probably an advanced user who knows all this information already, or you have opened somebody else's document. If the latter, open a new, blank one.

Click on the down-arrow next to the 'Normal'. You should see a list of options, including the Styles we mentioned above.

Play around with your document for a while. Type a few lines, then select different options from the drop-down list and see how the format changes. What you are doing is applying Styles. These Styles have been pre-formatted by Word, and you could use them just as they are. This will give you a lot of functionality and you won't have to worry about setting up your own. If this is the route you decide to take, move on to page 31 which talks about setting up the few styles you may need which do not come by default, or to page 34 where the discussion moves on to other things that can be done with existing Styles.

Setting up styles

If you want to create your own styles, go click Format>Style. You'll get a dialogue box with a long list of styles (see Figure 2.8). In fact, there may be a bewildering multitude of them. The best thing is to ignore most of them, and just focus on the ones we mentioned above.

For instance, select 'Normal'. At this point, it will be set to the Microsoft Word default – probably in Times New Roman font. Somewhere in the dialogue box will be an exact description of how that style is formatted. But there will also be a button called 'Modify'. This is where you can change practically everything about the style you have selected.

For the 'Normal' style, let us decide that you prefer Arial to Times New Roman. Click 'Modify'. A new dialogue box pops up on top of the previous one. One of the buttons at the bottom of it will read 'Format ...' Click on it and you will get more choices. You want to change the font, so the choice is obvious. Once you have clicked on 'Font', a further box with selections appears. Simply pick the font face and size you want, and click 'OK' when you are done.

Then be careful! You are now back in a previous dialogue box and you are just about to fix the format of that particular style. To make sure it 'sticks', you must tick the little box that says 'Add to Template'. Only then, click 'OK' again, and then 'OK' for the last time.

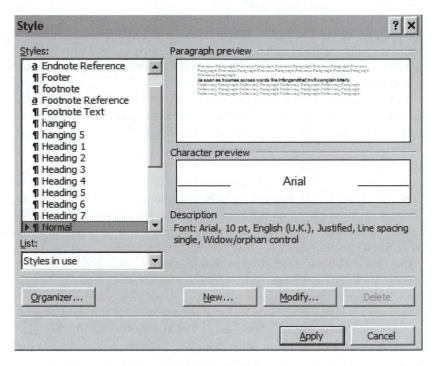

Figure 2.8 The Style dialogue box.

If you had several paragraphs based on the 'Normal' style in your document already, they should all have changed now to reflect the changes in formatting you chose.

We have said that many Styles in Word are automatically pre-set. You might be tempted to ask 'Where are they pre-set, and how?' Similarly, you might want to know where the changes you make to the styles are actually saved. The answer to both is the same: in a so-called **Template**. A Template is probably best described as 'a layout document which represents what Word thinks a basic document should look like'. It has pre-set margins, fonts, and paragraph styles. When you create a new document, it is always automatically based on such a template.

You can see what is going on if, instead of simply clicking on the New Document icon in your toolbar, you select File>New ... If you do that, you are offered a selection of types of documents you might want to create. What you are actually seeing are templates, of which you select one.

Add to template

The default template, in Word, the one that is applied behind your back unless you actively do something about it, is called the 'Normal' template (or, for the technically inclined, 'normal.dot'). You can create your own templates and call them something else. You can also back your templates up, which is highly recommended if you have added a lot of styles and other customisations. You do this by simply locating your template and copying it to a floppy disk, CD-ROM or other removable device.

For the time being any change you make to a Style is saved in the template that is currently open (usually your 'Normal' template), **as long as you tick the 'Add to Template' box**. If you do not do that, the Style will still be added to that particular document, but the formatting will be vulnerable and may, under certain circumstances, disappear.

Once you have successfully formatted the Normal Style to suit your taste, do the same with at least three Heading styles (we recommend 1, 2 and 3). Consider Heading 1 as the one you want to use for major chapter headings, Heading 2 as the one for sub-headings, and Heading 3 for sub-sub-headings. Most scholars do not go much further than that, but if you need another one, you can always format it later.

One important thing to remember for Headings is that you always want to keep them with the text that follows – it will look odd if your Heading is on page 59, and the text it relates to starts on page 60. There is a part of the formatting process for paragraphs which lets you set this. If you go through the usual Format>Paragraph routine for your style, look for the tab saying 'Line and Page Breaks' which is somewhere close to the top of the resulting dialogue box. In that box, make sure that 'Widow/Orphan control' is ticked for *all* paragraph styles you create, and that 'Keep with next' is ticked for every Heading style you create (see Figure 2.9).

Widows and Orphans

Widows and **Orphans** are old printing terms denoting standalone lines which are abandoned far from the rest of the paragraph they belong to. A 'Widow' is a line that has been left behind on one page when the rest of the paragraph is located on the following page. An 'Orphan' is a single line which is on the page *after* the page which contains the rest of the paragraph. Both look somewhat sad, and professional publications avoid them. By ticking 'Widow/Orphan control' you ensure that your styles automatically adjust paragraph formatting to avoid them, too.

'Block quotation' and 'Bibliography' are probably not listed yet, so you will create them from scratch. To do that, simply click in a paragraph which you want to be a block quotation. Select Format>Style again. This time, instead of Modify, click New (see Figure 2.10).

You will get a dialogue box with a number of interesting fields. In the one called 'Name', simply type the name for your Style. It can be anything you like – let us assume you are choosing 'Block quotation' here. In the 'Style Type' box, 'Paragraph'

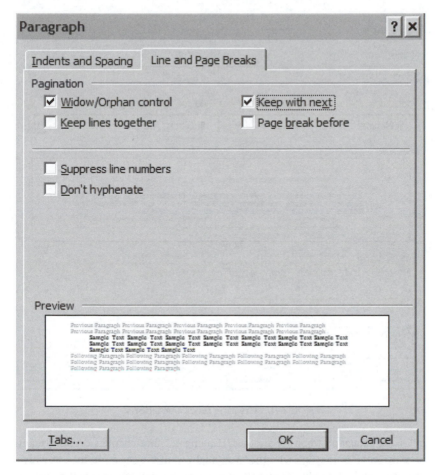

Figure 2.9 Widow and Orphan controls.

is usually the correct format to choose, and your intuition will tell you when this is not the case.

'Based on' is important. For any paragraph which is part of your main text (block quotations or bibliography included) and even for footnotes, the style they are based on should be your 'Normal' style. What does this mean? It means that the basic formatting is exactly the same as for your standard text, and all you then need to do is to add in (via 'Format' at the bottom of the dialogue box) the little bits that set it apart, that make it different.

Equally important is 'Style for following paragraph'. This sets the default for whatever the next paragraph after the one you are just dealing with is going to be. For instance, if you were formatting 'Heading 1', you probably would not want your

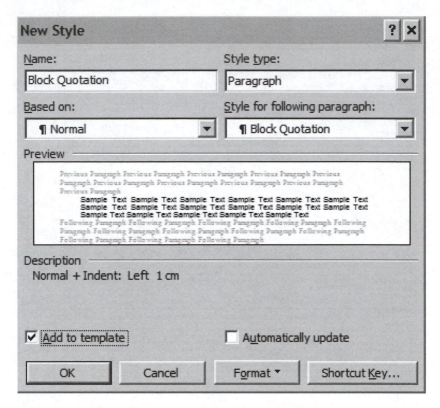

Figure 2.10 Creating block quotations.

following paragraph to be yet another 'Heading 1', since chapters do not usually have two titles following each other. You might want it to be a sub-title, in which case you could set it to be 'Heading 2' by default. Or you might decide that you are more likely to follow it with plain text, and in that case you'd set the default to 'Normal'. You can of course always override the default in your actual document, simply by choosing another style from the drop-down list in the top left corner.

For a Block quotation, the most suitable paragraph to follow is probably either another Block quotation paragraph, or a Normal paragraph. Whichever you decide, select it from the list in this dialogue box. Then tick the 'Add to template' box.

These were all preliminaries. Now you can actually format your Block quotation style. Click 'Format' again (still in this dialogue box), and select 'Paragraph'. Remember that you only need to focus on the things that you want to be different from a Normal Style, since Normal is already your base. So you don't need to do anything to the font face or size, since you would not normally change these for a quotation.

Block quotations are usually indented on the left side, and sometimes even on the right. You should therefore choose an indentation that you consider suitable. Remember, if it looks strange in the end, all you need to do is change it once in the style itself and all the paragraphs based on it will update automatically. There is no reason not to be adventurous.

Since quotations are also usually single-spaced (and your main text, your 'Normal' Style, should be set to 1.5 spaced at the very least), you have to change the Line Spacing box to 'Single'. And you may want to add a few points of spacing both before and after your quotation. Four points or 6 points on each side is usually plenty (see Figure 2.11).

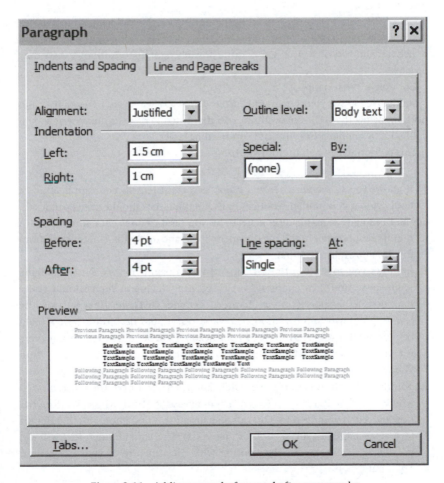

Figure 2.11   Adding space before and after paragraphs.

Your document outline – moving material around the easy way

This is where you reap some more rewards of your hard work.

You have set up your styles. You have saved your template. You are typing your text and you are applying the styles as appropriate: Normal is the default for your entire text, and you are using Heading 1 for chapter headings, Heading 2 for sub-divisions of chapters, Heading 3 for the level below that.

This lets you do clever things. Assume that your document is 60 pages long and, because it is still just a draft, it is in somewhat of a mess. You think you really want to rearrange the order of the chapters, but in a 60-page document, it is hard to know what is where.

Click View. Select Outline. To start with, nothing much would appear to change, but you now have a new toolbar, one which has arrows pointing right and left, and which has numbers on it: 1, 2, 3, 4 ... quite possibly right up to 7, though there may be gaps.

Click on 4. What happens?

Suddenly, you see your chapter headings *only* – you see levels 1 through 4, and nothing below that. This view shows you the structure of your document as you defined it by applying heading and sub-heading styles.

This is enormously helpful for two things:

1. It allows you to see whether you have been consistent in your application of levels. And if you suddenly notice that something that should have been a sub-sub-heading is a sub-heading instead, all you need to do is click somewhere in that line (but do *not* highlight the entire line), and apply the correct style from the drop-down list, as usual.

2. It allows you to shift entire sections of your document very easily. Imagine your sub-section 2 in chapter 3 on Good King Such-and-Such should really have been a sub-sub-section in chapter 1. Set your **Outline View** to show the levels right down to the section you want to shift, but no more. There should be plus or minus signs in front of your headings, depending on whether there is text associated with them or not. Mouse over the one in front of the section you want to move, until the cursor turns into a kind of cross with four arrows pointing in each direction. Then click, and hold. Now drag the entire line to where you feel it really belongs. Then release it. Your whole section has now moved. If you need to, you can also promote it or demote it to a different level (e.g. chapter to sub-section or vice versa). The actual hidden text will not be affected – you are simply working with the structure of your document. Try it out.

▶ How to make a 'Table of Contents'

While looking at the Outline View, especially if you already have many sections and sub-sections, it may have occurred to you that what you see there looks almost like a Table of Contents.

The truth is, if you have been conscientious about using Styles with your headings, you can get Word to automatically create a Table of Contents for you, complete with page numbers, simply by using those styles that you have applied.

Click Insert. Select 'Index and Tables'. Then pick the tab that says 'Table of Contents' (see Figure 2.12).

You will get a wide selection of options. Most of them will be very obvious to you. The ones to watch out for are under 'General', towards the bottom of the dialogue box.

In 'Formats', you will probably want to select one of the pre-set formats, not the 'from template' option. The reason is that in your template, chapter headings are likely to be formatted quite large and bold, which isn't really necessary for a table of contents. Check the others and see what you like, or click 'Modify' and create your own.

In 'Show Levels' you can select whether your Table of Contents shows only the main chapter headings, or levels of sub-headings, and how many. You are likely to

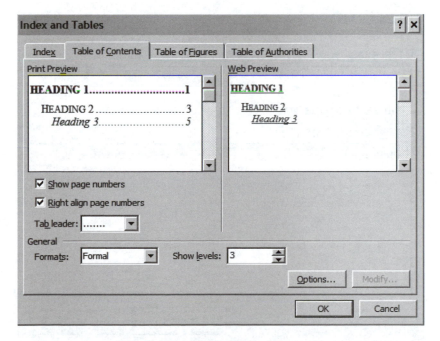

Figure 2.12 Adding a 'Table of Contents'.

want to show everything, so set the level figure high enough to cover all the levels you have.

▶ Bookmarks and cross-referencing

You will be relieved to hear that this has nothing to do with Styles. In fact, it is a function which is very easy to use and is extremely convenient if you have to cross-reference within a long dissertation.

Assume the following: you have written an outline of your dissertation and on what is currently page 1, you know that you want to refer to something which is currently on page 46, but which may, once you have added some more text, well end up on page 143 instead. You could wait until you have written the entire document and then remember to check and insert the correct page, but there is an easier way.

It is a two-stage process.

First, on page 46 highlight the first words of the text you want to reference (or if it is a footnote, highlight the footnote marker).

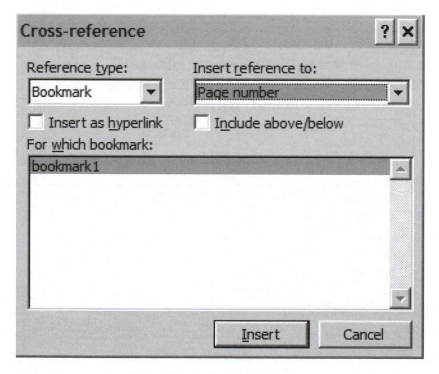

Figure 2.13 Bookmark dialogue box.

Choose Insert>Bookmark ...

Give the **bookmark** a name that will help you remember what it was about.

Click 'Add' and then close the dialogue box.

Second, go to page 1. Click wherever you want the reference to appear. You might, for instance, be typing a the sentence 'The curious incident of the duke and the duck will be more fully elucidated below, on page ...'. Instead of the three dots, place your cursor at the end of that line.

Now choose Insert>Cross-reference ... You will get the dialogue box displayed in Figure 2.13.

It lets you choose from a wide variety of things you can reference, and different ways of inserting that reference. It is worth clicking the drop down lists simply to check these out. For now, however, select 'Bookmark' as your Reference type, and select 'Page number' as the referent.

This will result in the following appearing magically on your screen:

'The curious incident of the duke and the duck will be more fully elucidated below, on page 46'

If you click on the 46, you will notice that it is a field. It may even let you jump straight to the section referenced. But the best thing about it is that it will update no matter where the referenced text moves to, and you can stop worrying about it now.

▶ Making a backup of your document template

If you have spent a lot of time customising your styles, you don't want to lose all that hard work, so make sure you back up your template occasionally.

Under normal circumstances, your template is called **normal.dot**, and it is hidden deep in the user data on your system. There is an easy way to find it, though. First, make sure Word is *not* open. Click on your Start button (in Windows), then select Search>For Files and Folders. Type 'normal.dot' into the search box which appears, and start your search. Normal.dot will come up very quickly. Highlight it when it shows up, and copy it to a removable device just like you would any other file.

▶ Presentation using Powerpoint

Powerpoint has become so ubiquitous that the mere mention of it is often greeted with a groan. Hours spent watching presentations by hapless presenters who read off the bullet points in their presentation one by one have given rise to the phrase 'death by Powerpoint'.

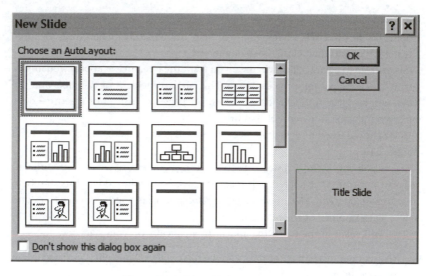

Figure 2.14 New Slide dialogue box.

But there is no need for a Powerpoint presentation to be boring, because the software gives you a multitude of options; you can go well beyond bullet points and integrate just about anything else into it.

Of course there will be reasons to have slides with bullet points – after all, they can lend structure to your talk (nice for your audience) and serve as reminders of what should come next (nice for you). The main thing to remember when presenting is *not* to repeat the text on them; they serve as a guiding rail, not as content. For the same reason, keep them brief and snappy.

In its basics, Powerpoint works a lot like a word-processing package – only the document is called a 'slideshow' and each page is a 'slide'. The way most people use slides is by having a slide title and some bullet points on each. However, much more interesting than bullet points are the other things you can do.

When you first create a slide, you are presented with the 'New Slide' dialogue which offers you a choice straight away (see Figure 2.14). Do you want a chart, a graph, a picture, a table? You do not have to choose straight away, though, since you can still insert (or delete) these things later if you change your mind. This is what we are going to deal with next.

Using Images and Draw Objects

Assume you have a blank slide, or a slide which had bullet points on it which seemed, ultimately, too boring to you, so you deleted them.

To put anything else on the slide, click Insert> ... and marvel at the possibilities presented (see Figure 2.15).

Figure 2.15 Insert menu.

Now imagine, first of all, that you want to use a plain image – a picture of a historical figure or of a historical location, or a map. For historians, maps make particularly useful Powerpoint features. You can click Insert>Image>From File … and navigate to any image you choose that happens to be on your hard drive. Suppose that you use a map of your area of study. Select it, and it will appear on your slide. You will be able to manipulate the size of the image by clicking on it and then dragging the sides or the corners.

Animating an image

You can use the Custom Animations feature (see Figure 2.16) to make this map appear on a mouse click, or you can even set a timer which will make it appear automatically,

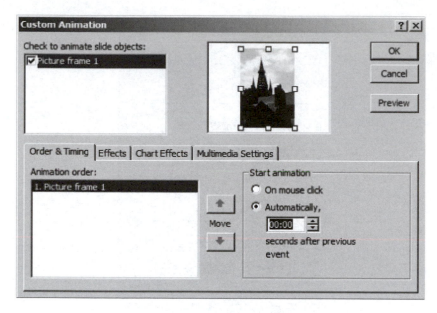

Figure 2.16 Managing an animation.

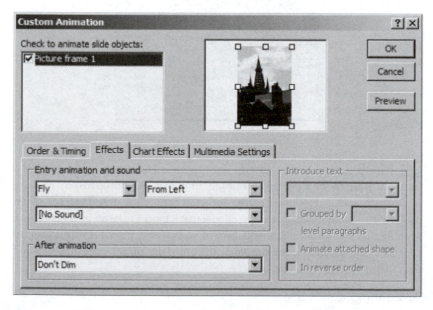

Figure 2.17 Adding special effects to an animation.

a certain number of seconds after the previous event (which may be a slide transition or another mouse click).

You can also determine how exactly it appears – whether the map simply blinks in, or uses any number of clever (sometimes too clever) modes of appearance. Check the 'Entry Animation Options' in the 'Effects' tab of the Custom Animations dialog box (see Figure 2.17).

You will see that you can also set a sound to be associated with the image, and you can decide what you want the image to do after the following mouse click.

We recommend that you do not go overboard with all these features. Use the ones that will make your point best, without distracting your audience.

Once you have your map there, you can use other Powerpoint features to demonstrate a variety of things. For instance, you may want to show particular hotspots where certain events took place, or movements across a landscape, or boundary lines, or the locations of certain types of buildings.

Draw Objects

To do this, the Draw features (usually located in a toolbar at the bottom of your screen, but this may vary from version to version) are invaluable (see Figure 2.18).

These allow you to paint dots, lines, boxes, and a variety of other shapes on the picture. You can use several of them, you can manipulate their sizes and colours, you can write in them and you can set their Custom Animation to make them appear either on a mouse click, or in a timed sequence. This takes some getting used to and you have to be prepared to spend some time investigating all the possibilities, but here is a simple example.

You have a map, and you want to highlight two specific locations on this map. First you want to talk about the map all by itself, so you do not want the two locations to show up. Then you want to highlight the first site, and talk about that for a while. Next you want the second one to be presented.

First, insert your map. You do not need to animate it, since it is the first thing you want the slide to show when you get to that point.

Next, use AutoShapes in the Drawing Toolbar to draw a circle. To do this, click on the Oval once, then click and drag on your slide. Don't worry if you are not exactly in the right place – you may move the object later. Also, bear in mind that by holding down the shift key, you can make sure that the oval always turns into a perfect circle.

Figure 2.18 Draw Object toolbar.

Next, right-click your new circle and select 'Format AutoShape' from the menu (see Figure 2.19).

This brings up a dialogue box (see Figure 2.20) which will let you format the circle in any way you like, including its fill colour, the colour of the line around it, the thickness of the line around it, and, if you investigate the other tabs on this dialogue box, its size and various other items, too.

Also note the little box at the bottom of the dialogue box which gives you the option of setting your selected format as the automatic format for new objects you create. If a circle is set to have a green fill by default, but you know you will always want yellow, you can click a green circle once, select the yellow fill, and then tick this box to set it as the future default.

Once you have made your settings and left the dialogue, your circle should look exactly as you want it.

Highlight the circle, and hit Ctrl-C, then Ctrl-V. This copies it – after all, you want two circles, and if you've already gone to the trouble of formatting one, why create a new one from scratch?

Now move the circles to their final locations.

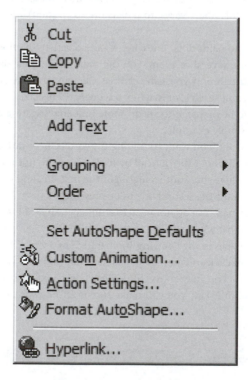

Figure 2.19 The Edit menu.

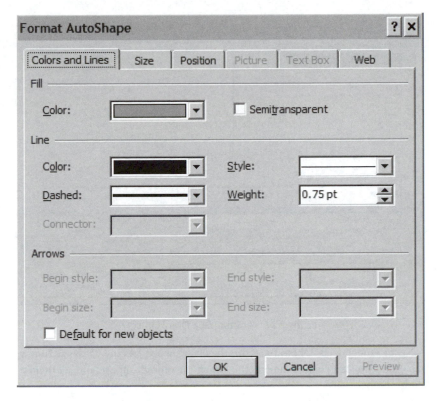

Figure 2.20   The Format AutoShape dialogue box.

Animating Draw Objects

With the slide looking the way you want it to be at the *end* of whatever you are going to use it for, highlight the first of the dots you want, right-click it, and select 'Custom Animation'. Do not worry too much if you change your mind about the order, since you will be able to adjust anything you like at a later date.

You will see a dialogue box, usually displaying the 'Effects' tab first, which lets you select the objects you want to animate. (See Figure 2.21.) As you tick them, they will show up in the little display box to the right.

Below this, you see the options for the kind of animation you want. In most cases, it is cleanest just to choose 'appear', but you may wish to experiment with more spectacular modes of entry.

Next, you select what you want the object to do after it has appeared. Most often, you would probably want it to stay on display, so you would select the 'don't dim' option, but you may decide to have the image disappear again.

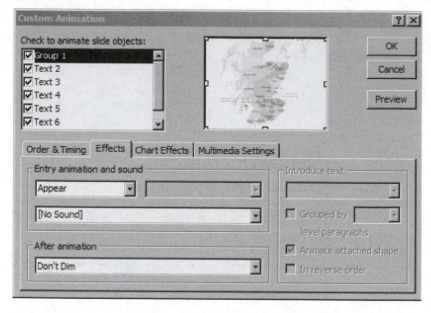

Figure 2.21 Animating a Draw Object.

Next to the 'Effects' tab, to the right, the dialogue box has the 'Order & Timing' tab. Here, you can change the order in which the objects appear, and set them to do so automatically.

In later versions of Powerpoint, you can run a test within the Custom Animation dialogue itself. For other versions, leave the dialogue, run Slide Show, and see how it is presented.

You may use these techniques with any kind of background and any kind of Draw Object. You can also use them with text, although the text will have to be contained within a Draw Object.

To do this, simply create any Draw Object – a box, a circle, an oval – and set both the 'line' and the 'fill' to transparent.

After clicking on a Draw Object once, you can write text in it. This is not always necessary or appropriate, however. If you do write text in a Draw Object, remember that you can change font face and size, too. Simply highlight the text and use the toolbar at the top of your screen, just as you would in Word.

Once you have done this, you can animate the object, and the text will be animated with it.

A different kind of 'Order'

An important feature for those who want to use several objects on a single slide is the 'Order' menu entry on the right-click menu for objects. If several objects overlap

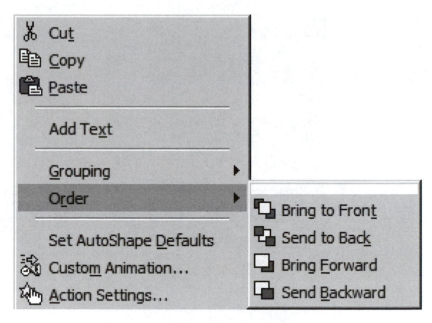

Figure 2.22   Ordering objects.

(be they dots on maps or arrows on images) you will of course want to make sure that the correct one is on top of the other. There is no point in having a map with dots if the dots end up behind the map where, despite the best animation, nobody will be able to see them. This often becomes an issue where the order of appearance of objects is changed: suddenly what was at the front originally should now be at the back, and the question is how to get it there.

Right-click on your object. Or, if the object in question is now hidden behind a large other object, click on the large other object. Select 'Order ...' from the menu that appears (see Figure 2.22). This will give you four options: you can send your object forward or backward by a step each time, or you can send it all the way to the front or to the back with a single click.

Grouping

Sometimes you may want to make sure that the various objects you have placed on your slide stay together, or move together, as a unit, even though they were created separately and could, in fact, be completely different types of object – for instance an image and a Draw arrow.

To achieve this, you can use a feature called 'grouping'. It is also located in your Drawing toolbar, but often inconveniently hidden behind a button that simply says 'Draw' on it, at the left of the screen.

Figure 2.23   'Ungrouping' objects.

First, highlight all the objects you want in the group together. To do this, click on one of them, then hold down CTRL as you click on the next, and the next, and so on. Once you have them all highlighted, release CTRL.

Click Draw, then select 'Group' at the top of the menu. That is all you need to do. The objects will now move in a group. You can also resize or animate them as a group. To undo the action, choose 'Ungroup' from the same menu (see Figure 2.23).

Organisation charts

The possibility of using organisation charts is worth a brief mention here because they can be used to display very basic family trees. The rather significant proviso is that the chart as contained in the program was made for businesses; for this reason, presumably, it does not allow for lateral relationships to have a joint dependent. In plain terms, this means that you cannot show a father and a mother

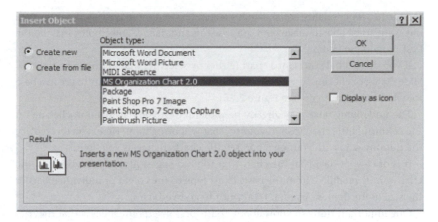

Figure 2.24   Organisation charts.

linked, and have the child joined to the middle of that link. If you are content to only display one ancestor, however – for instance, follow the paternal line only and ignore marriage relationships – the chart works quite well.

Your first step is to select the Organization Chart layout from the New Slide – Auto Layout dialogue. If you are not starting a new slide, click Insert>Object, and select MS Organization Chart 2.0 from the dialogue box (see Figure 2.24).

NOTE: The Insert>Object dialogue is well worth investigating no matter whether you want an Organization Chart or not, since it gives you a good idea of many other things you are able to do. For example, you can import files from other applications such as Word or Excel, or insert video and audio files.

Once you have selected the Organization Chart, you will see a basic chart appear which you can fill in and to which you can add. You can change more or less everything about this chart – the background colour in the boxes, the font of the writing, the words in the title. If you want to change colours and fonts, the easiest way to do this is to click somewhere in the white space outside the actual chart and drag the mouse all over the chart, to highlight all the elements. Then you can use the top menu bar to make your changes.

To add more elements, click on one of the five options in the toolbar, and then click on the chart element you want to assign it to. Once you have an element in the chart, you can also **drag and drop** it.

Using graphs in Powerpoint

Powerpoint allows you to insert graphs and charts to visualise data. In many ways, this is very similar to what spreadsheets let you do (see Chapter 5). The difference is that in Powerpoint, the mathematical functionality is much reduced, while the formatting functionality is somewhat greater. If you don't have very complex data but want to be able to make your graphs sing and dance, Powerpoint may be the best program to choose.

If you decide that you want a chart (either by selecting that option from the New Slide dialog or clicking Insert>Chart), you are given a dummy chart to use as a base for what you want to do (see Figure 2.25).

The underlying table may already be presented to you – if it is not, clicking on the colourful little chart icon in your toolbar will bring it up. Here, you can replace the dummy data with your own and see the chart change as you do it.

It is once your data is in the chart that the fun starts. Almost everything in the chart can be modified, from the basic chart type to the colour of individual bars or the size of the figures. Again, it is best not to go overboard.

One important thing to know about charts on Powerpoint slides is that they are in a container of their own – the 'Chart Area'. When the chart is just sitting on the slide and you right-click, one kind of menu comes up – the same menu as for any other object (like, e.g. a Draw Object). You can use this menu to animate the chart (though not components within it); and to cut, paste and do the usual things you do to objects.

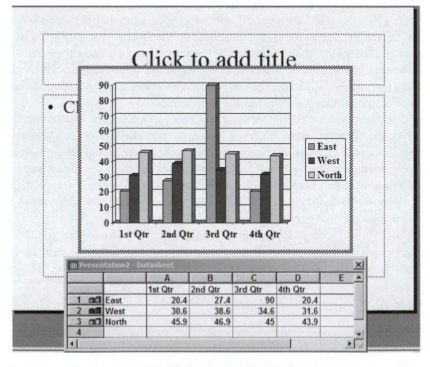

Figure 2.25   Inserting graphs.

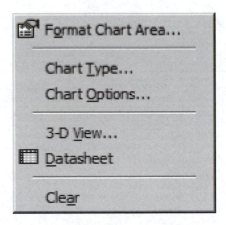

Figure 2.26 Formatting charts.

Once you have double-clicked the chart, it will not look much different, but there will be a black line all around it. You are now in the Chart Area. Right-clicking here will bring up a completely different menu (see Figure 2.26).

From this menu, you can change the chart type and access a great number of options which include labelling on the different axes, labelling of individual chart bars, legends and titles.

Finally, you can manipulate the chart directly. Clicking once on any element will usually select all the elements of that kind. Clicking again (not double click, just two separate clicks) will select that element alone. Right-click, and investigate the menu that appears.

Most problems with manipulating charts in Powerpoint arise because users are trying to do something while in the 'wrong' area, so the correct menu does not appear. If you encounter this problem, try double-clicking your chart first, and then trying again.

Getting onto the World Wide Web

Just like with Word, anything you have on a Powerpoint slide can be formatted to serve as a **hyperlink** out to the Web – always provided that the computer you present on is connected to the internet.

Highlight the text or image you want to employ as a link. Next, select Insert>Hyperlink. This brings up a dialog box which gives you a number of options (see Figure 2.27).

In Powerpoint 2000, you can browse to a page you have recently viewed, you can select from a list of links which are in your computer's memory, and so on. In earlier

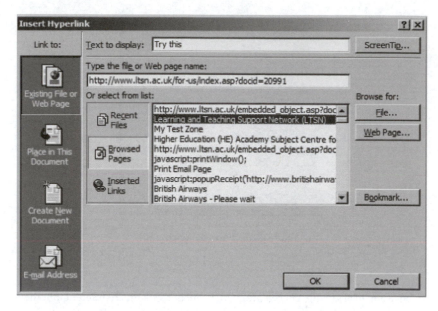

Figure 2.27   Putting slides on the World Wide Web.

versions of Powerpoint, you do not get so many options, and the simplest way to insert the hyperlink is to go to the webpage you want first, highlight the URL in the address bar, and hit CTRL-C for copy. This means you will have it ready to paste into the Insert>Hyperlink dialogue with CTRL-V.

What not to do with Powerpoint

Powerpoint is a very versatile program, and it is easy to get caught up in all the options and forget that it is only there to assist and support your presentation. It offers multiple options for making your point visually, but there is the danger of creating overload in your audience. Just like doing nothing but read off bullet points is a sure way to send your audience to sleep, so also, having something blinking and flashing on every single slide is certain to get them annoyed and ensure they lose the thread of your argument. It is a good idea to play around with the program for a while to become familiar with what it can do, but in the end, its flashier elements are best used sparingly.

Another important thing to bear in mind is that you will have to operate the program in a foreign environment, with an audience. Make sure that you know exactly how all your slides work, and that you have established with the venue that all the facilities you need (including a compatible version of the program, an internet connection if you plan to go online, and a drive that will take your portable medium of choice) will be available. Do not show up with your presentation in Powerpoint 2002 on a CD Rom to find that the machine at the venue runs Office 97 and only has a USB port.

▶ Guide to further reading

Benjamin, Jules R., *A Student's Guide to History*, ninth edn (Boston and New York, 2004).

The Chicago Manual of Style, 15th edn (Chicago, 2003).

MHRA Style Guide: A Handbook for Authors, Editors, and Writers of Theses (London, 2002) also available at http://www.mhra.org.uk/.

Page, Melvin E., *A Brief Citation Guide for Internet Resources in History and the Humanities*, available at http://www.h-net.msu.edu/about/citation/.

3 History on the World Wide Web

The **World Wide Web** (WWW) is a library of resources available to computer users through the global **internet**. The Web and the internet are often used interchangeably but strictly speaking the internet is a collection of computer networks which communicate directly with each other and the World Wide Web is the library of resources available via the internet. By the end of 2002 there were more than 100,000 networks and over 120 million users connected via the internet. Internets support a range of different services. A few of the most popular include:

- **E-mail** (electronic mail): allows messages to be sent from one person to another, or to many others, via computer.
- **FTP** (File Transfer Protocol): is a set of standard conventions allowing the easy transfer of files between different computers.
- **User groups**: allow the automatic global distribution of messages among thousands of users who are members of particular interest groups.
- **Telnet**: is a system that allows a user to 'log on' to a remote computer.

The Word Wide Web is also an internet service. It enables users to view a wide variety of information, including archives, library resources, and current world and business news. Users generally navigate through information on the Web with the aid of a **program** known as a **browser** or client. The browser displays text, images, sound and other information in the form of a page, which is obtained from a WWW server. The user can navigate through information by pointing to specially designated hypertext or other objects on the screen. These objects link the user to other Web pages on the internet. Web pages are formatted using Hypertext Markup Language (HTML). The World Wide Web was developed by Timothy Berners-Lee at the CERN research facility near Geneva in 1989. Originally it was to allow information-sharing among teams of physics researchers.

This chapter will consider the use of the World Wide Web by historians and discuss:

- Subject directories
- General directories
- Search engines

- Evaluating information found on the Web
- Archives
- Other online resources
- Plagiarism and the Web.

► History and the World Wide Web

If you want to use the World Wide Web for your history studies, you should first of all think about why, and what you are hoping to find. There are of course worthwhile resources on the Web, but unless you know where to find them, the chances are that you will come across a lot of junk while looking for them.

History resources on the Web can be divided into three main kinds:

- Sites which are written to give information about a historical topic, much in the way a textbook or article might be written.
- Sites which provide access to source material about a historical topic, much in the way an archive might.
- Sites which are set up to encourage reflection on a historical topic through a combination of pre-written information and exposure to original source material.

The first and third kind can often be located by using search engines and subject directories. The second kind is harder to find, though subject directories can provide useful guidance.

The first kind of site also has to be treated with extreme caution, but by applying the right critical skills you will soon be able to tell when you can or cannot trust the information on a site.

► Finding history sites

If you are starting from scratch, you will probably be using either a **search engine**, a **general directory** or a **subject directory** to find sites about the topic you are interested in. Subject directories can be a very useful first start, particularly if your subject is one of the better-known ones. Search engines have wider coverage, but will inevitably throw up some questionable results. General directories are somewhere in between, but tend to be less useful for more obscure subjects.

► The difference between subject directories, general directories and search engines

Subject directories

Subject directories are often maintained by government-funded agencies, academic institutions or libraries, though occasionally you will come across one which is maintained by a lone enthusiast. If you are only just beginning to locate material for your subject on the Web, a subject directory is probably the safest place to start. You may also discover that all the sites you might otherwise have painstakingly collected for yourself with individual internet searches have already been brought together by an enterprising soul and are presented to you on one handy page.

The following is a list of a few of the main subject directories in history. It is by no means exhaustive, but this selection should offer a good starting point, and other subject directories are generally linked from these sites.

The WWW Virtual Library – History Central Catalog [http://www.ukans.edu/history/VL/]: An index of history-related sites, maintained as an integrated and international network of indexes. Its central catalogue provides direct links to network sites. Each index is maintained by volunteers who are familiar with the needs of scholars and instructors in the area for which they are providing links, and who aim to establish standards of coverage and selectivity that will make their sites effective tools for practising historians wishing to work on-line.

Internet History Sourcebooks [http://www.fordham.edu/halsall/]: Thousands of **copyright**-permitted resources as well as links to more specific subject portals. In order to keep them copyright free, the resources themselves tend to be somewhat old – for instance, nineteenth-century translations of relevant literature rather than more up-to-date twenty-first-century ones. As such, the documents may be useful for general guidance or, as they are frequently used, for teaching, but for serious research you would probably have to go elsewhere. Still, the sheer mass of resources hosted at, and linked from, these pages make a visit worthwhile.

The HUMBUL Humanities Hub history section [http://www.humbul.ac.uk/history/]: Humbul is part of the Resource Discovery Network, and it provides a catalogue of evaluated online resources in the humanities, targeted principally at the Higher Education constituency. The resources are grouped into subject areas, of which History is one. It also contains other sections of interest to historians, including Archaeology, Classical Studies and Celtic Studies.

The British Academy Portal [http://www.britac.ac.uk/portal/]: This is the British Academy's directory of online resources in the humanities and social sciences. It is designed as an entry point to available resources for those working in higher education and research.

In addition to these resources, there are two directories which are of particular use for medieval studies:

The Labyrinth [http://labyrinth.georgetown.edu/]: The Labyrinth provides free, organised access to electronic resources in medieval studies through a World Wide

Web server at Georgetown University. It offers connections to databases, services, texts and images on other servers around the world.

The ORB – Online Reference Book for Medieval Studies [http://www.the-orb.net/]: The ORB is an academic site, written and maintained by medieval scholars for the benefit of their fellow instructors and serious students. All articles have been judged by at least two peer reviewers. Authors are held to high standards of accuracy, currency and relevance to the field of medieval studies. The site maintains an Encyclopaedia, Library, Reference section and Links section.

The best way to use a subject directory is simply to follow the links that interest you from the main page, or to type your area of interest into the search engine which many of these directories now have. The directories have all been compiled by an expert (or at least enthusiast) in the field and are likely to yield valuable results with little effort on your part.

Directories

Like subject directories, general directory sites are maintained by people who attempt to categorise the sites they find and omit websites which are clearly useless from their list. They are not, however, run by subject experts. In addition, they tend to have a much wider remit and their audience will not be academic. Most directories are run by commercial organisations which try to draw as many users as possible in order to sell advertising.

They still perform a useful weeding-out function, but the drawback is that you have to rely on somebody else's judgement regarding the quality of a site, and you do not know how far you can trust that judgement.

The best-known directory site is probably still Yahoo! [http://www.yahoo.com/] (see Figure 3.1).

Search engines

In contrast to directories of any kind, search engines do not work with human input. Their results are compiled from indices created automatically by programs (called bots or spiders) which run through the Web and investigate the content of every page they find. When a search term is typed into a search engine, these indices are scanned to bring up the results.

The content of the pages indexed by a search engine is not evaluated. Until a few years ago, this meant that to find anything relevant, users had to either spend a lot of time checking search engine returns one by one, or come up with ingenious search terminology to eliminate as many 'false returns' as possible.

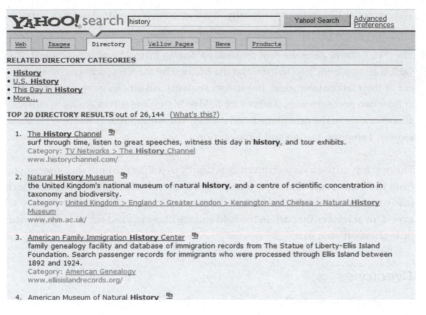

Figure 3.1 The Yahoo history pages.

Despite this, if you are looking for something very specific, a plain search engine, used intelligently, may be of greater use and yield results more quickly than scrolling your way through a directory. Because search engines are automated and their bots crawl over the Web day and night, search engines also record new sites much more quickly than directories which rely on humans to notice the site, evaluate and enter it into a database.

Nowadays, improved **search algorithms** have made the search engine route slightly less of a gamble. Still, knowing how to make sure certain terms are *not* included in a search, or how to tell a search engine to look for words in a particular order, remains a useful and timesaving skill.

The most effective search engine has for a number of years been Google [http://www.google.com/]. It has become so popular that 'googling' or 'to google' has become a standard term for searching something on the Web. Google pioneered an improved search algorithm which did not just scan for the presence of search terms in a website, but also checked whether a particular site had been linked from other places and thus considered useful by other people. It is a complicated ranking mechanism, and at the time of writing, it works.

However, there are ways of making it operate with even better results, and to do that, it helps to know how a search engine really works.

How a basic search works

If you type **oh say can you see** into your search box, most search engines will go and look for sites on the Web which include *any* of these words – whether just one, two or all – in *any* kind of combination. They can appear in complete isolation any- where in the text. Since these are all fairly common, nondescript words, you will get a wide range of returns, none of which may be particularly relevant to what you are actually trying to do. (Google is an exception here since they use a different method.)

This happens because the default for most search engines is to assume that when you type **oh say can you see**, you mean 'give me *oh* OR *say* OR *can* OR *you* OR *see* or any combination of these anywhere in the document in question'.

+ − " * or: how you can make it work better for you

However, what you probably want to tell it is that you are looking for *oh* AND *say* AND *can* AND *you* AND *see* in that particular order and combination. Fortunately, there is a way of doing that.

If you have an entire phrase, like the one above, to search, put double quotation marks (*not* inverted commas!) around it. A search phrase with quotation marks around it is called a **search 'string'**. By using search strings, you can ensure that the returns only include websites which contain the words you asked for in the par- ticular order in which you submitted them. Therefore, if you type "*oh say can you see*" into a search box, you are likely to find the lyrics of the United States national anthem within the top returns.

You may also want to bear in mind the fact that some subjects may be indexed under a number of variants. Names are particularly tricky issues. You may be looking for "**franklin roosevelt**," but the most important website dealing with him may refer to him as "franklin d. roosevelt" throughout, so that your "**franklin roosevelt**" search string would not bring it up in the results. If one string doesn't get you anything useful, therefore, bear variants in mind. Try "**franklin delano roosevelt**," or even **FDR** (capitals here to avoid returns on random letter combi- nations in the middle of words) if you get desperate enough.

If you don't have an exact phrase to look for, you can still control the output by using + in front of any word that is essential to your search; for example, if you only want to see sites which contain both the word *birds* and the word *bees*, type **birds +bees**. This will ensure that sites which talk about birds, or bees, alone will not be among the returns. Using AND in front of words instead of + will have the same effect: **birds AND bees** works the same way as **birds +bees**.

But perhaps the most important thing to be able to do, is to tell the search engine to leave things out. Take an example of looking for information about Scottish cas- tles. Unless one is able to tell the search engine specifically to exclude terms such as 'luxury holiday' and 'Mary Queen of Scots', the first hundred results are likely to offer package tours to every single one of the hundreds of castles in which Mary Queen of Scots is supposed to have rested her weary head, but in reality never did.

This is where the minus sign '−', or the term NOT, comes in handy. If AND is used to force the search engine to include things, NOT is used to force it to omit terms. These terms are called '**Boolean Operators**', after the binary approach to logic developed by the nineteenth-century mathematician George Boole. Using them, you could have a search called:

> **"scottish castle" NOT holiday NOT "mary queen of scots."**
> or
> **"franklin roosevelt" AND "sally hemings"**

Or, taking a different example:

> **"roman amphitheatre" +gladiator −"russell crowe."**

Bear in mind that these techniques can also be very helpful when searching for material within online archives.

If your search engine offers an **Advanced Search** option, this is a good way to do essentially the same thing. In addition, you may have a choice of language for your search returns, you will be able to say whether a site that is more than two years old is still of use to you, and you can choose whether or not to include formats other than HTML in your returns (see Figure 3.2).

Other search engines such as AltaVista [http://www.altavista.com/] or Excite [http://www.excite.com/] offer similar functions to the Google 'advanced' search page.

A final useful tip for searching, is the use of the wildcard, or '*' character. Suppose you are looking for information about oppression of the working classes in the nineteenth century. Documents of relevance might indeed include the word **oppression** but then again, they might be using **oppressed** instead, or talk about the **oppressor**. The wildcard character '*' lets you look for all three in one go.

Simply find the part of the word that all these terms have in common. In this case, the common denominator is **oppress**. Using this, with the wildcard attached, will send a search engine to search for any word that starts in **oppress**, no matter how it continues.

A useful search for this kind of topic might therefore look something like this:

> **"nineteenth century" OR "19th century" AND "working class*" AND oppress***

Finally, a note about capitalisation. The main thing to say about capitalisation is that it *limits* the search. If, in a search, you type everything in lowercase, the search engine will by default bring up results in lowercase, uppercase, and everything in between. This gives you the widest range of results.

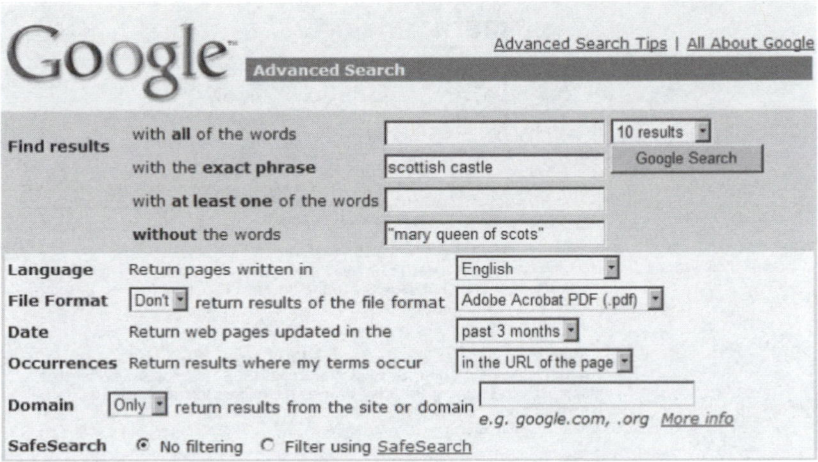

Figure 3.2   The Google advanced search page.

If you capitalise a letter, or an entire word, the search engine will then look *only* for instance of that word which has the same combination of capital letters and lowercase letters as you entered in the search box.

Sometimes this can be useful, for instance, if you really want to know only about the Civil War, and not about just *any* civil war. At other times, it is safer to do without capitalisation to start with.

Useful search engines and directories

When looking for information, you should first make up your mind which way might be quicker and more effective for you. If you are looking for a broad topic, directories are usually a good place to start; if you are looking for something very specific or unusual, a search engine will get you to the information more quickly.

If you want to go the directory route, Google Directory [go to http://www.google.com/options/index.html and select 'Directory'], the Open Directory Project [http://dmoz.org/] and AltaVista [http://www.altavista.com/dir/default] are very comprehensive, user-friendly and well established. Yahoo! [http://www.yahoo.com/] is also well established and comprehensive, but it contains so much advertising that it is hard to find the relevant sections. On the Yahoo! front page, the directory currently lies below the first screen which is full of other, less relevant things.

As for search engines, the best one currently available is Google [http://www.google.com/]. AltaVista have introduced a Google-like minimalist interface to their search function at http://www.altavista.com/ (note that to get to the directory you now have to click on a tab at the top of the logo).

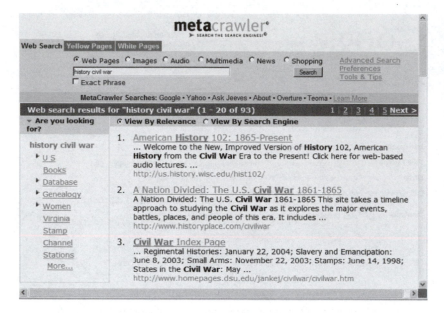

Figure 3.3 A Metacrawler search.

A search engine which is potentially very useful for academics in particular is SearchEdu [http://www.searchedu.com/]. It only returns websites which are hosted at academic institutions among its results. This is not foolproof, since there are potentially many websites with first-year undergraduate essays out there, but it is definitely worth a look.

It is also worth knowing about meta-search engines. These will submit your query to several search engines at a time, and some will group the results according to categories. Metacrawler [http://www.metacrawler.com/] for example, will search Google, Yahoo, Ask Jeeves, About.com, and some other search engines concurrently and list the result categories in a bar down the left hand side of its results page (see Figure 3.3).

▶ Evaluating information on the World Wide Web

So this is how you find sites – even to some extent, how you make sure you are likely to find the most relevant site. However, this still leaves you to establish how useful or more importantly, trustworthy, any given site is.

This section applies to the kinds of websites which purport to give you the essential information on a historical subject, not to archive sites which simply offer resources for you to study and make up your own mind.

One of the wonderful things about the Web is that anybody can make information available quickly and without too much expense, and anybody else will be able to locate it relatively easily. But this is also one of the deeply problematic things about the Web.

There are many conscientious, intelligent people writing material and putting it online. There are also many crackpots. Worse, there are many who are completely sane and well meaning, but simply not trained to academic standards and they present their view of the past as though it was the established truth. And some of them are very literate and very convincing.

Therefore, the problem of evaluating the usefulness of websites and their content is a major issue.

It has to be said straight away that in some respects, this is no different from the problem of evaluating any other publication. The difference is that school and undergraduate study trains us to distinguish academic publications from non-academic ones on the same subject (though of course there are borderline cases, and there are also people who never quite get the distinction right). The training takes place imperceptibly and relies on our understanding of the markers and conventions of the various forms of publication, our comprehension of the authorities behind these and whether or not they are relevant to academic research. We know that a feature in a popular history magazine is probably more superficial in its approach than an article in a peer-reviewed history journal. We know that paperbacks entitled *On The Trail Of (insert historical character's name here)* are, in all probability, less academically reliable than a Yale biography of the same person. Somehow, somewhere, we have picked these things up and internalised them. Whether conscious or not, criteria have been established in most people's minds by which they judge the likely value of a print publication even before they have read it.

On the Web, however, some of these criteria no longer hold. It is hard to find the HTML equivalent of glossy magazine format versus bound-in-leather book format. The authority lent by a respected publisher's name is often no longer present. New authorities are being established and it is unclear what the criteria for them should be.

However, it is still possible to make value judgements about websites and their content, and some of these criteria are very similar to those you use to evaluate print publications. One just has to look for them in different places, and sometimes they do not look exactly the same. In addition to this, it is possible to build up a reasonable set of criteria based upon common sense.

Since this is a recognised issue, a number of Web pages deal with it in a variety of ways. First of all, and specifically for historians, there is *Internet for Historians* [http://www.vts.rdn.ac.uk/tutorial/history], part of the HUMBUL Virtual Training Suites. This is a free, 'teach yourself' tutorial that lets you practise your Internet Information Skills.

Another interactive tutorial is the *'Internet Detective'* [http://www.sosig.ac.uk/desire/internet-detective.html] which lets you practise evaluating the quality of internet resources.

Another very good site which includes examples of reliable and unreliable websites, and even a quiz is the *Guide to Critical Thinking About What You See On The Web* [http://www.ithaca.edu/library/Training/hott.html]. It also offers an extensive bibliography.

Finally, for those who prefer to work with a simple list of criteria, some of the most useful are the *Evaluation Criteria* published by Susan Beck at New Mexico State University [http://lib.nmsu.edu/instruction/evalcrit.html] and *Thinking Critically about World Wide Web Resources* by Esther Grassian at UCLA [http://www.library.ucla.edu/libraries/college/help/critical/index.htm]. Both sites offer very comprehensive lists of criteria which have been valuable for the discussion that follows.

The keystones of website appraisal can be said to be: **Accuracy, Authority, Objectivity** and **Currency**. As an academic, you will be primarily concerned with establishing whether or not the information you find on a site is accurate. The other three points, Authority, Objectivity and Currency, while important in their own right, could first and foremost be considered indicators as to whether the information you find is *likely* to be accurate or not.

Accuracy

So how do you judge the accuracy of what you find?

Well, how do you judge the accuracy of something somebody tells you in a book? There are three pointers you can use:

- prior knowledge of the material
- internal consistency of the site's (or book's) content
- established indicators (for books, peer review or recognised publishers; for websites, the three subsidiary points mentioned above).

If you have done preliminary reading on your subject (always highly recommended), you are clearly in a very good position to judge whether a site contains enough accurate information for its new assertions to carry some weight with you. If it contradicts much of what you already know, you will be wary of trusting its new assertions. If it conforms to the things you already know, you will be more prepared to add any new information, albeit cautiously, to the list of things you may consider accurate.

In addition to this, you will also be able to judge whether the site gives enough information about the topic in question; if you have prior knowledge, you will be able to tell if crucial parts are omitted, and whether all sides of an argument are shown.

However, it is possible that you come to a site unprepared. In that case, here are some basic things you might ask yourself about it.

- Is it clear who wrote the content? Is there a name, and is it even vaguely familiar? Are there contact details? (If so, you may want to contact them with follow-up questions.) Does the author give information about his or her educational qualifications, or the background from which they approach the subject? Official qualifications do not necessarily mean trustworthiness, and neither does lack of qualifications mean that an author doesn't know what they are talking about, but it is reasonable to want to know the angle from which they are approaching the subject.
- In addition to an author, is there a site editor? Some sites bring together contributions from a number of authors, specialists in individual subjects. If there is an editor, is a form of peer review in place, and is it explained? Who *is* the editor? And if a site has neither author nor editor information, are you not entitled to wonder why they are so keen on anonymity?
- What is the aim of the site? Is it stated clearly anywhere, for example in a mission statement or in something as simple as an introduction? Does the content of the site match its avowed aim?
- Do the spelling, grammar and composition conform to accepted standards? If that is not accurate, do you trust their ideas?
- Do the external links lead to sites you know to be trustworthy? Do any trustworthy sites link to this one? Has anybody reviewed the site?
- Is the information given verifiable? Does the writer quote sources? Are the sources themselves known to you, and are they respectable? Have you been able to check any of them out? Does the author use the sources responsibly – that is, do they quote sources according to their spirit, or do they quote misleadingly or out of context?

A site does not have to fulfil all of these criteria to be considered respectable or useful, but if you have to answer 'no' to more than a couple of these questions, you should definitely treat it with caution and try to verify its claims elsewhere.

The next question to consider is that of authority.

Authority

Looking for signs of 'authority' is a time-honoured way of getting a feeling for whether or not a book is likely to be academically valuable or not. You check which press has published it, who the review editors are, where the author is employed and what their qualifications are, and whether any known names are endorsing it. This very traditional approach to evaluating quality is not always valid with regard to web-based information. A person can have very thorough knowledge and worth-while ideas without having their book, or site, published or hosted by a recognised institution. However, as a rule of thumb, looking for indications of institutional support for a site can do no harm.

Ask yourself:

- Where is the site hosted? Is it in an educational **domain** (e.g. .ac.uk or .edu) or any official domain (e.g. .gov), or is it hosted by a commercial organisation (e.g. .co.uk, .com, .net)? Is it hosted on one of the free Web servers to which any-body can sign up? or even by GeoYahoo, a free server which will host pages from anyone at all (geocities.com)? You can tell by looking at the **last** part of a site's address before the **first** single forward slash.

Examples:

The Internet History Sourcebooks are at http://www.fordham.edu/halsall/. The first single forward slash is between 'edu' and 'halsall'. Thus the last part of the domain address is '.edu", an educational domain in the United States.

The history section of the Arts and Humanities Data Service is at http://ahds.ac.uk/history/. The first single forward slash is between 'uk' and 'history'. Thus, the last part of the domain address is '.uk' – in this case, all that it tells you is the country where the site is hosted, so you go back a little further, and look at the part before that. Here you have '.ac'. The '.ac.uk' together tells you that the site is hosted by an educational domain in the United Kingdom.

- Where does the content come from? Sometimes, publications which were previously in print are scanned and put on the Web. This can be a good thing (see e.g. the project Gutenberg): [http://www.gutenberg.net/index.shtml]; the Electronic Text Center [http://etext.lib.virginia.edu/]; or the Online Medieval and Classical Library [http://sunsite.berkeley.edu/OMACL/]. Sometimes it means that an outdated (and therefore out of copyright) publication has been placed onto the Web – it may be useful in some respects, misleading in others. If the content of a Web page was not originally created for the web, can you tell where it came from? Did it come from a print publication, from a course handout, an undergraduate essay or from notes scribbled on a beer mat?
- Does the site carry advertising? Educational sites generally will not – but then again, neither will sites hosted on commercial servers, as long as the site owner pays enough. Therefore, the presence of advertising is only a general guide. Check how much there is, and by whom. The more advertising, the less seriously the site should probably be taken. The nature of the advertising is also important – is the advertising unrelated to the content and simply there because the site owner did not pay for an advertising-free site? Or are you being targeted

to buy items directly related to the site content? If the latter, be particularly careful.

• Who, if anybody, sponsors the site, and what might their agenda be? Sponsorship is just a more subtle form of advertising. Of course there are respectable reasons for sponsoring a site. Just bear in mind that this is an issue worth considering.

This last question leads to another issue – that of objectivity.

Objectivity

This is a vague area where you may have to rely on your own judgement, but it is no more difficult than dealing with a dubious academic article. Simply use your common sense, and some of these questions:

• Does the content of the site sound like special pleading? Do you keep wanting to go 'But …' as you read it?
• Can you detect a clear bias in how things are presented?
• If there is bias, is it openly stated? Bias doesn't mean that a site is useless – published academics are biased, too, even if they deny it. But it does mean you have to be more wary of accepting anything you find at face value.
• Does the author of the site at least acknowledge that there are two sides to an issue (most historical issues have at least two sides)? Or are they trying to sneak something past you?

The final criterion is much easier to pin down – currency.

Currency

The Web is a constantly growing medium. It is quite easy to put up a website cheaply and quickly. This means that some people do it without much thought, remain enthusiastic about that site for a while, then move on to the next project in a different domain. And the original site remains, especially if it was hosted by a free server with advertising.

This means that you may come across a site that looks very useful, but was last updated in 1996. This is not a problem if you are dealing with an archive of older material, but it is an issue if the site promotes views which have since been refuted by further academic study and debate.

These are some means by which to tell the currency of a page:

• Is there any indication when it was first put online, and (more importantly) when it was last updated? Some webmasters – the people who create the website and make it available for general view – are conscientious about including this information, but many, especially amateurs, are not. If there is no indication, you can find a little program (an **'applet'**) at http://www.bookmarklets.com/ which will tell you anyway.

- Do the external links on the site in question still work? If many links are dead, the site may be quite old, and it is most definitely of less use than it could have been. If there is an e-mail link to the author, does that still work, or has the author moved on?

Miscellaneous considerations

These are some additional observations which are difficult to make into hard-and-fast rules. Take, for instance, the format of the page. What is the colour scheme? Is it easily readable? Is it funky and flashy or is it staid and boring and, well, face it, academic? Is the font consistent?

What is the ratio of advertising to content? We have mentioned advertising in the section on authority, above. There it served as a pointer to who might hold a stake in the site and its contents. But there is another side: does the advertising actually outweigh the content? Do things flash and blink, does the site spawn sub-windows all over the place, and does it try to deploy dozens of **cookies** (small pieces of information that track your usage) on your machine? If it does all this, would you buy a used car from the author? Would you trust their historical assertions?

While academics may have atrocious taste and may also get carried away with clipart, content is generally the main focus of truly educational sites, and distractions will be few.

In the end, there is one crucial question left: Should you be here at all? What kind of information are you looking for, and do you think the Web is really likely to provide it? Would you find your information more quickly and reliably elsewhere – in the library, for example, or in a reference work? The Web is a useful repository of resources, but depending on your subject, it may have less to offer than traditional resource collections.

▶ Archives

Useful resources you find on the Web can roughly be subdivided into three kinds:

- reference material such as indices, catalogs and bibliographies;
- primary source material such as documents, texts, databases and images; more recently also sound and video;
- secondary source material or 'written history', for instance full-text journal articles.

The traditional location for both primary and secondary source material is the Archive, whether of journals or of databases, text and images, and this is one type of resource collection which is progressively moving online. Where, even a decade ago, you had to travel to remote places, carry a letter from an academic to apply for a reader's card to let you into the hallowed halls which sheltered fragile manuscripts from the hands of the mundane, and sit inhaling dust for six weeks in your summer vacation; sometimes now all it takes is an archive search and a facsimile or transcription of the document that you desire will appear on your computer screen. Failing that, it is often possible to order photocopies or scans of archive material online, and the digitisation of archival content is progressing at considerable speed.

Unfortunately, material held by online archives does not usually appear in a search engine search, nor is it normally catalogued in directories. You have to know that the online archive exists, and then search for the material within it. This is where the 'reference' type of resource becomes important. Archives are often badly publicised, but indices and catalogs help you locate them. One invaluable site is: http://sunsite.berkeley.edu/Libweb/ at the University of Berkeley, which offers a comprehensive list of online libraries worldwide. Other websites which tend to provide valuable information about newly available online resources are:

Google Scholar [http://scholar.google.com/]: Google Scholar is a relatively new service which lets you search specifically for scholarly literature, from articles to books and theses. It is constantly growing and is probably at the forefront of development right now.

JSTOR [http://www.jstor.org/]: JSTOR is dedicated to helping academics take advantage of advances in IT, by archiving scholarly journal literature for improved access, gap-filling, preservation and reduction of library costs. It is worth checking back often to discover what new materials have become available.

H-Net [http://www.h-net.org/]: H-Net is run by scholars for scholars and was set up to develop the educational potential of the Web. H-Net publishes a range of materials, from essays to multimedia, and is a good place to find out what's new in the world of academia and IT.

In addition, here are some links to some major online archives, and also to a few sites which list currently existing online archives.

- *Library of Congress Online Catalog* [http://catalog.loc.gov/]
- *The National Union Catalog of Manuscript Collections* [http://www.loc.gov/coll/nucmc/nucmc.html]
- *The Public Record Office/National Archives Online* [http://www.nationalarchives.gov.uk/]
- *The Australian Dictionary of Biography* [http://adb.anu.edu.au/moreadb.html]

- *Access to Archives*, which in 2004 contained 6.9 million catalogue entries from 351 English record offices and other repositories [http://www.a2a.org.uk]
- *The Scottish Archive Network* [http://www.scan.org.uk]
- *Institute of Historical Research* [http://www.history.ac.uk]
- *British Library* [http://www.bl.uk]
- *HUMBUL* [http://www.humbul.ac.uk/history] – use the Primary Source Search with your own search term
- The 'Archives' page at the WWW *Virtual Library for History* [http://www.ukans. edu/history/VL/bibliography/archives.html]
- *Historical Abstracts and America History and Life*, both [http://serials.abc-clio.com] – note that this is not a free service.
- *The Wilson Indexes*, offering journal databases in full-text, abstract and index format [http://www.hwwilson.com/default.cfm]. See particularly the *Readers Guide* at [http://www.hwwilson.com/databases/Readersg.htm]. However, note that this is not a free service.
- *ProQuest Historical Newspapers project*, offering digitised newspapers from the nineteenth century to the present [http://www.il.proquest.com/proquest/ features/feature-04/default.shtml] – note that this is not a free service

Where services are not free, you are in luck if you are studying at an institution that has subscribed to them. It is usually difficult for individuals to obtain (or afford) a subscription.

Sometimes, all an archive website does is let you access the archive's catalogue. You will still have to order photocopies or scans, or travel to the archive itself, but at least you will know that the archive actually holds some material that is of relevance to you.

Other archives make selected material available online, and as digitisation projects proliferate, the volume of this material is bound to grow considerably. Most frequently, searching an archive will be very similar to using a search engine, and Boolean Operators will be particularly useful.

▶ Sound and film archives

A type of historical resource which is gradually becoming more widely available is digitised film and digitised sound. A good starting point for accessing such material is the *Library of Congress Digital Collections* and *Programs page* [http:// www.loc.gov/library/libarch-digital.html]. In particular, you may want to look at the *American Memory Historical Collections* [http://memory.loc.gov/ammem/ index.html].

In the United Kingdom, the *British Universities Film & Video Council* [http:// www.bufvc.ac.uk/] and *Education Media Online* [http://www.emol.ac.uk/] provide access to a large and growing number of film and sound recordings to anybody accessing from a UK higher or further education institution.

▶ Other useful online resources

The JISC Resource Guide for the Arts and Humanities [http://www.jisc.ac.uk/ index. cfm?name=rg_artshum_main&x=16&y=11]: A guide to a range of resources set up by the Joint Information Systems Committee in the United Kingdom to meet the needs of teachers and students in the arts and humanities. It includes:

- Bibliographic, reference and research information describing, and linking to, 17 individual searchable databases which cover history material.
- Full text publications which can be viewed online and saved by users, including eighteenth-, nineteenth- and early twentieth-century pamphlets in Social Policy and Transport History, and a digital archive collection of core scholarly journals.
- Subject gateways including the HUMBUL Humanities Hub.
- Digital resources in a range of data types, incorporating historical data collections from the late tenth to the twentieth century, non-fiction film and video, marriage and mortality statistics, and a number of image collections.

COPAC [http://www.copac.ac.uk/copac/]: COPAC provides free access to the merged online catalogues of the British Library, the National Library of Scotland, and 24 of the largest university research libraries in the United Kingdom and Ireland. You will not be able to download much material, but you will find out where books are held and therefore where to go to, or order them from.

AHDS History – the history section of the Arts & Humanities Data Service [http:// ahds.ac.uk/history/]: The Arts and Humanities Data Service (AHDS) History section collects, preserves and promotes the use of digital resources, which result from, or support, historical research, learning and teaching. You can use data freely for your own personal research. Its collection is eclectic since it depends largely on the resources academics submit to it. AHDS History also has sister sites devoted to archaeology, literary, linguistic and other textual studies, the visual arts and the performing arts.

Palaeography [http://paleo.anglo-norman.org/]: An excellent teach-yourself website for medieval and early modern palaeography.

The British Humanities Index [http://www.csa.com/]: This site is only accessible to those in possession of a valid ATHENS Password. If you are a member of a university, you may be able to get one from your library. The British Humanities Index is a database listing abstracts from over 400 academic journals and other publications since 1962. It contains more than 650,000 entries and is constantly growing. Other sites available via ATHENS include: JSTOR [http://uk.jstor.org/] a database of back issues of over 500 full text journals in Arts & Sciences, Business, General Science, Language and Literature, and Project Muse [http://muse.jhu.edu/], a database of over 250 full text journals from around 2000 to date.

▶ Book-marking a site

Once you have identified a site as useful for your studies, you don't want to lose it again. Set a 'bookmark' for easy access in future. If you are using Internet Explorer, you do this the following way.

First, make sure you are on the page that you want to bookmark.

Click 'Favorites'

Select 'Add to Favorites'

Now you will get a dialogue box which presents you with various options (see Figure 3.4).

Pay attention to the 'Name' field. This will contain whatever the creator of the website considered a good title for the site. Sometimes it is very useful. Sometimes

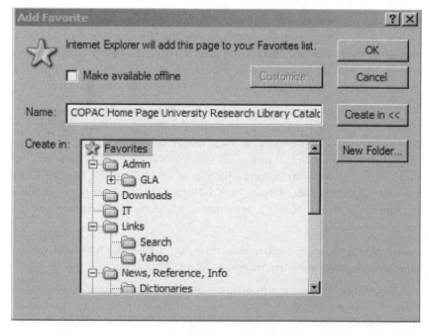

Figure 3.4 Book-marking a website.

it is too long, uninformative, or simply not what you want. Use the field to give the site a title that works for *you*.

Also, pay attention to the 'Create in' button. If it shows two arrows pointing to the *right*, click on it and it will expand the dialogue box to show you some more, very useful, options. (If the arrows point to the left, it is already expanded and you should be seeing something very similar to Figure 3.4.)

If you are book-marking many sites, you may want to group them somehow. To do that, click on the 'New Folder ...' button. You'll get a new dialogue box overlaid on the previous one, which invites you to create a folder. You might want to choose a name such as 'History Sites'. Once you have clicked on 'OK', the new folder will show up in the main dialogue box. You can then click on any of the folders in the larger 'Create in:' window, click 'OK', and the address of your site will be saved, with the name you have given it, in the folder you assigned it to.

Next time you want to go to it, simply click 'Favorites', run your mouse down to the folder in question, and follow the arrows to the right.

▶ Plagiarism and the World Wide Web

The internet offers an array of resources for historical study, but has also helped to increase levels of plagiarism. There may be a great temptation to cut and paste a paragraph from a webpage and place it directly in an essay or dissertation, but copying from the internet as with any other source constitutes plagiarism. Plagiarism is considered as cheating by most institutions and therefore care should be taken to acknowledge Web sources (see Chapter 2 for information on this). There are now programs available to check documents for unacknowledged copying.

▶ Guide to further reading

Cameron, Sonja, *Evaluating Internet Sites for Academic Use*: http://hca.ltsn.ac.uk/resources/Briefing_Papers/bp2.php
Condron, Frances and Cooper, Grazyna, *Internet for Historians*: http://www.vts.rdn.ac.uk/tutorial/history

4 Historical Databases

This chapter explores the creation, analysis and dissemination of databases based on historical sources. A step-by-step approach for the creation of databases is provided, taking readers from the original source to the completed database. The second section of the chapter concerns data analysis and information retrieval covering querying one table or more than one table; sorting and viewing information; using statistics; and grouping and cross-tabulating information. The key methodological problems facing historians translating sources to database are outlined and the chapter ends with a brief discussion of some of the recent developments in database technology.

▶ What is a database?

A **database** is an organised or structured collection of information. Any compilation of related material, whether computerised or not, could be termed a database. The information or data could exist in an ordered form, for example, an address book or a table of football results. Alternatively, the information could be largely unstructured, for example, a diary or political pamphlet. The data need not comprise wholly or partly of text but could also be a set of images, sounds or moving pictures. Confusingly, the term database is also used to signify the software that manipulates the data. In strict terms, this should be known as a **database management system** and it is this software which allows the querying, manipulation and retrieval of information from the original source material.

It is possible to construct simple databases from a wide range of historical documents as many sources already possess an implied or evident structure. Most obviously, these are sources which are already organised in lists. Examples of such sources are census enumerators' books, freeman's rolls, parish records, electoral registers, school admissions books, shipping records, trade union membership lists and so on. It is also feasible to create databases from less structured sources, for example, probate inventories and wills, court records including depositions, obituaries, newspapers, and so on. This type of database is often referred to as a **free text** or **free form** database. The digitised text may be supplemented by other media including images, film clips or sound. There is more information on free text databases in Chapter 6 (pp. 135–137). A third type of historical database may be assembled from a range of related material. The most obvious example of this type of database is a **prosopographical** study: a selection of biographical data collected from various sources on connected individuals, perhaps councillors, governors, members of parliament or even actresses. Therefore a prosopographical database may contain columns containing names, addresses, education, religion, occupation, and so on.

The most straightforward database is one based upon a single **table** (or **flat-file**). The table consists of columns or **fields** and rows or **records**. The example in Table 4.1 depicts a flat-file database of the census for the village of Harbury in Warwickshire of 1881. The fields include: ID numbers for individuals and households, first name, surname, age, sex, marital status, occupation and birthplace. Each record contains a complete set of information for one individual within the census, in this case, the separate members of the Checkley household.

The advantages of a flat-file database are its ease of use and the fact that it is possible to utilise the database functions of most spreadsheet programmes as well as database management software in order to analyse the database. This allows the user access to the statistical and charting functions of spreadsheets as well as some data analysis (see chapter 5 for more information on using spreadsheets as databases). For simple querying, searching, sorting and viewing of data this may be the best solution for sources which are not too complex. A flat-file database may be compiled from one source, or many, as long as the information translates to a simple columnar table. The Harbury Census as depicted in Table 4.1 is an ideal example of such a database. However, as soon as the information provided in the source (or sources) becomes more complicated, or supplementary information is provided, the single table model becomes clumsy and unworkable. For instance, the flat-file database would be unable to link the names in the 1881 census, either with a later census for the same town or with other related sources such as electoral registers or rate books for the same period. In some cases, trying to structure the source material so that it will fit into a single table model means creating tables with vast numbers of columns, many of which remain empty. In these situations a multi-table approach should be adopted for ease of **data entry**, for maintaining accuracy, and to facilitate analysis.

Although there are competing models for using multiple tables in a database the most common type today is the relational model. Data is organised in an infinite number of related tables. The tables are linked together by having common elements. For example, in Figure 4.1 a model for a **relational database** has been constructed from seventeenth-century English assize records. There are five tables each with links to one or more other tables. The *Defendant ID* field links defendants to a **Sentence** table and an **Offences** table. A **Witnesses** table is linked to the **Offences** table via the *Case Number* field. There is also an **Occupational**

Table 4.1 Harbury census of 1881

Household ID	Person ID	Dwelling	Census place	Source	First name	Surname	Condition	Age	Sex	Relation to head	Occupation	Birthplace
39	150	Church Street	Harbury, Warwick, England	FHL 1341742 PRO RG11	Edward	Checkley	Married	67	M	Head	Farmer 67 acres	Harbury, Warwick
39	151	Church Street	Harbury, Warwick, England	FHL 1341742 PRO RG11	Elizabeth	Checkley	Married	55	F	Wife	Farmer's wife	Blakesley, Northampton
39	152	Church Street	Harbury, Warwick, England	FHL 1341742 PRO RG11	Edward S.	Anderton	Unmarried	24	M	Son-in-law	Farmer's son	Sydney, Australia
39	153	Church Street	Harbury, Warwick, England	FHL 1341742 PRO RG11	Anne L.	Anderton	Unmarried	13	F	Daughter-in-law	Farmer's daughter	Blakesley, Northampton
39	154	Church Street	Harbury, Warwick, England	FHL 1341742 PRO RG11	John	Checkley	Married	74	M	Brother	Farm servant (indoor)	Harbury, Warwick
39	155	Church Street	Harbury, Warwick, England	FHL 1341742 PRO RG11	Ann	Checkley	Unmarried	36	F	Niece	Domestic servant	Mollington, Oxford
39	156	Church Street	Harbury, Warwick, England	FHL 1341742 PRO RG11	William	Sheldon	Unmarried	15	M	Servant	Farm servant (indoor)	Cubbington, Warwick

Source: Harbury census database.

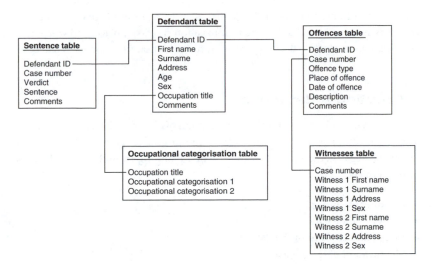

Figure 4.1   Assize records database illustrating links.

Categorisation table linked via the *Occupation Title* field in the **Defendant** table. Relational tables allow a great deal of flexibility and adaptation and therefore may be used for a number of different purposes.

Some historians have rejected a tabular approach to database design and analysis because of the compromises that have to be made when fitting historical documents into a rigid structure. This has led to the development of the **source-oriented** approach to the computerised analysis of historical sources. With this strategy the complete source is entered onto the computer and categories for analysis are decided later. The main advantage of this approach is its flexibility. For example, the database will deal with the non-standard, pre-modern units of measurement and currency: non-standard dates such as St. Mark's Day or 'Rent day' can be interpreted even if they take different forms in different geographical regions; as all coding and categorisation takes place *after* data entry the database can be used by many different researchers for different purposes; and sources which do not easily translate into a tabular form can be analysed without making concessions because of a rigid database structure. However, the increased flexibility of the source-oriented approach comes with a cost. The databases are time-consuming to create and complex to analyse. There are also fewer software solutions available commercially and the most successful source-oriented databases are those that have been created by academic historians. Text analysis packages can be used for this type of analysis but do not offer all the potential of bespoke solutions. It should also be remembered that *any* database is merely a representation of an historical document so whether the translation is to a relational or a source-oriented database the historian is always one step removed from the original. Therefore, what is important is that the database creator is aware of how that process of translation has taken place, and where necessary can document the decisions taken in the transition from source to database.

▶ Creating a database

The more systematic the approach to the creation of a historical database, the easier it is to modify or refine that approach as the project progresses. Therefore, the following steps should be kept in mind when planning to undertake a database history project:

- Planning the project
- Analysis of the data
- Design and creation of the database
- Modification of the database
- Data entry
- Querying the database
- Data documentation.

These steps may not necessarily be sequential, and for example, the design of the database may change in the light of experience of data entry, but they do give an outline of the process.

Planning the project

At its most basic, the planning stage involves deciding on the project's objectives. For example, is the final outcome to be a resource which will be analysed by a range of users or, instead, a focused database to achieve a specific objective for one project? If the database is to serve a limited function – to answer a simple research question, for example – it may be possible to enter only a partial section of the original source in order to cut down on the resources required for data entry. For example, if the project objective was to research female employment in the nineteenth century, the database could contain simply women's names, addresses and occupations from the census enumerators' books. However, if the objectives were later expanded to research further questions on the family backgrounds, ages, and so on of the women involved, the database would have to be expanded and re-designed. Serious consideration should be given to the final product, even if the project has a limited objective. It is far more difficult to redesign a database and add data halfway through a project than to include it at the outset. In these cases, time saved at the start of a project may be, in fact, a false economy. The question of sampling the source should also be considered here. All historians use sampling strategies to some extent. For example, the study of a particular community or set of individuals targets a particular group or population. However, for very large sources time and budgetary constraints may require that the number of records studied is limited in some way. A sample may be **random** or **systematic**. Random sampling is a technique where a group of subjects (the sample) is selected for study from a larger group (the population). Each subject is chosen entirely by chance and therefore each member of the population has an equal chance of being included in the sample. By using random sampling the possibility of bias in the population is reduced. However, bias may be introduced by the selection method. Random sampling also needs some pre-preparation of the source. For example, an effective method of random sampling would be to allocate each record in a source a number. Then a random number generator (supplied with spreadsheets and statistical packages) could select numbers from a range to correspond with the numbered records in the source. Random samples also have the drawback that they are difficult to link to other related sources. For example, if a random sample was taken of individuals in baptism registers, then it would be necessary to examine entire marriage or death registers to search for those specific individuals. A parallel random sample of a marriage register may result in few matched records. Systematic sampling strategies include selecting records from a particular year or year(s) where a series of information exists; selecting every tenth or fifteenth record in a source; or letter-cluster sampling where names beginning with particular letters or combinations of letters are selected. Systematic sampling is more prone to bias. For example, the selection of particular surnames beginning with a certain letter may result in influential clans or families being included or excluded from a population. However, the advantage is that other sources may easily be matched to the sample.

Time scales need to be decided upon and the amount of time available may limit the scale and scope of the database project. At this stage, it makes sense to have a rough idea of design issues. For instance, will the sources translate easily to a database model? If not, how will the extra material be dealt with? Might there be data entry problems, for example, difficulties accessing or reading the source material? Contact archives, if necessary, to ascertain any problems with locating, accessing or copying the material. Comparisons should be made with other, similar projects as some of the design issues may already have been solved by other researchers. What resources are available to meet the project objectives? Are there issues of **copyright**? Copyright matters are particularly relevant if the database is to be made available to others, especially if a charge is to be made for its use.

A first draft of a project plan indicating specific project goals and tasks should be drawn up, although this may need to be revised many times.

Analysis of the data

Before designing the database structure, it is important to assess the data the table(s) are going to contain. A thorough analysis of the source material will result in an easier transition from source to database and may also start to throw up patterns or possible questions for further investigation. This scrutiny of the source material may take several forms:

1. The data should be broken down into components that groups information into objects or events. These could be information relating to a person, an organisation, a document, an object or a building, or to events such as a marriage, a transaction, the making of a will or an election. In database terminology these groups of data are referred to as **entities**. Thus our Assize records database (Figure 4.1) had entities relating to people: the Defendant and Witnesses tables and an entity relating to an event: the Offences table. Each entity or group of information identified from the original source will eventually form a table in the final database.

2. Once each entity has been identified, it is necessary to return to the original source and list the data associated with each. For example, the Defendant table has information on the first name, surname, address, age, sex and occupation of each defendant appearing before the assizes. The Offences table gives information on the date and place of the crime. This information will produce the fields for each table. The fields are also known as **attributes**. Each collection of attributes describe the properties of each entity. Figure 4.2 outlines the structure of a voter table from the Halifax election of 1832. The attributes for each voter are: ID number, first name,

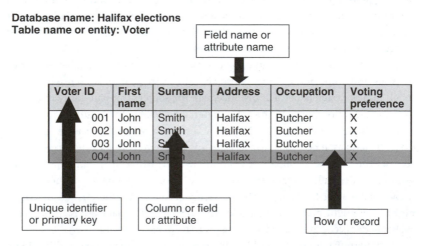

Figure 4.2 Voter table from the Halifax elections database illustrating basic database terminology.

Source: West Riding elections database.

surname, occupation and voting preference. Figure 4.2 also illustrates the basic database terminology.

3. Each field or attribute will contain information of a specific type. So, the next step in analysing the source is to consider the most appropriate type of field for each piece of data. Common field types for historical sources are described in Table 4.2. Issues that should be considered when allocating data types to information in historical sources include:

- Size: Take into account how large (in terms of numbers of characters) each field should be. Fields that are unnecessarily lengthy produce unwieldy databases.
- Calculations: Will it be necessary to perform calculations such as averaging and counting on the field? If so, the field type must be designated as numerical. However, often historical sources portray numerical information in non-arithmetical ways, perhaps a payment will be given as one groat, or a baby described as three days or six months old. In such cases the information in the source should be converted to a number.
- Dates: Will dates be allocated field types as dates or as numbers? In some historical databases it may be preferable to enter dates into three separate text fields, one for the day, one for the month and one for the year. This allows analysis to be undertaken on date-specific events and also handles the problem of missing information. Historians who are working with records before the standardisation of the Gregorian calendar need to adopt a strategy for managing dates. This standardisation took place in different countries at different times. In Britain, for example, the move from the Julian to the Gregorian calendar occurred in 1752. Some sources will use non-Christian calendars. The division of the year also varies from place to place. In some places the new year begins on 1st January, in others on 25th March. Some sources employ dual dating systems to satisfy the different local, regional or national practices.

Table 4.2 Common field types for historical sources

Text	For alphabetical or numerical data but beware that numbers will be treated like text if you choose this data type.
Numbers	For all numbers but you may wish to use one of the types below for currency/dates.
Date/Time	For dates and/or times.
Currency	In most commercial database software this is applicable only to modern currency.
AutoNumber	Allocates a unique identifier to each record. It is useful for ID fields.
Memo	For fields containing much unstructured information. Useful for comments fields.

- Currency: Pre-modern currencies are best broken into units and a field designated for each unit. Therefore, for old English currencies there would be separate columns for pounds, shillings and pence. If necessary, these fields may be converted by a formula to enable calculations to be carried out.
- Data that does not fit the specification: Often historical source material does not neatly fit into the field types and sizes allocated. For example, there may be occasional marginal notes or comments, large pieces of text or a piece of information which occurs too infrequently to be allocated a separate field. In these cases, the use of a comments column is helpful. Here, longer chunks of unstructured text may be stored or any extra information which does not easily fit into the database structure. It is good practice to include a comments field in each database. It may be removed at a later stage if superfluous. Alternatively, text may be entered into separate files and linked to the table.
- Unique identifiers: It is good practice for tables to contain one field or perhaps a small group of fields which identify each record uniquely. With historical records it is often difficult to find these identifiers from within the sources themselves. In these cases, it is useful to add an identification number to each record. These may be automatically generated by the database program which eases data entry and guards against any inadvertent duplication of numbers. Figure 4.2 illustrates the use of the unique identifier or primary key in the Voter table.

4. The next stage is to consider the relationships or links between the tables or entities in the database. Relationships may be divided into three separate categories: **one-to-one relationships, one-to-many relationships** and **many-to-many relationships**. One-to-one relationships occur when records in one table have only one match with records in a second table. Examples could be that a person dies only once and each death is of only one person. One-to-one relationships may usually be expressed in one table. One-to-many relationships are more common and occur when records in the first table match many in the second, but those in the second table only have one match. Examples could include an individual who owns more than one residence, but each of the houses is only owned by one person; or a mother who has many children, but each child has only one mother. Many-to-many relationships occur when records from both tables have relationships between them. For example, a person could belong to more than one club or society and each club or society has many members; or a local record that contains the names of a number of officials and these officials are in turn named in a variety of local records. Once a preliminary analysis of possible relationships has taken place, it should be determined if entities occur in one-to-many or many-to-many relationships. If so, the entities should be placed into different tables, and the relationships between the tables should form part of the database design.

These steps, in total are known as data modelling or entity relationship modelling and form an important step towards the creation of the final database.

Design and creation of the database

Once the source has been thoroughly assessed, it will be possible to sketch out the design of the database. Figure 4.1 gives a typical sketch for a database of the assize records. Once the structure has been sketched out, the next stage is to decide upon the number and names of the fields for each table, the type of data contained in each field, and the relationships between the tables. This information will enable the database to be constructed quickly and consistently. At this point, notes should be taken on the decisions taken and a brief outline of the reasons for those decisions. This documentation will prove to be invaluable if the database is to be accessed by other users, if others will be undertaking the data entry process, or if there is a delay between the database design and its later implementation. Once the database has been constructed, a pilot study should be undertaken, that is, a small number (perhaps 5–10) records should be entered into each table to ensure that the database will serve the purpose for which it was planned. For example, the information from the source material may not 'fit' into the field structures; the type of data contained in each field may need to be changed; or fields may need to be added as unanticipated pieces of information are discovered (although a thorough initial analysis of the data should mean that this will not occur). Some initial querying could also be undertaken at this juncture, again to see if the database is fit for its purpose. In addition, the pilot study will demonstrate if there are likely to be difficulties with data entry, due perhaps to the illegibility of the source material, and to estimate the length of time the data entry process will take.

Modification of the database

Once the pilot study has been completed, the database should be modified to take into account any difficulties or inconsistencies discovered. The database should continue to be assessed and modified if necessary until a robust and stable model has been constructed.

Data entry

Data entry is often the most time-consuming part of the database construction. However, it is also the most important. The design may be excellent, but if the completed database contains imperfect or error-strewn information, then any results acquired from the project will be meaningless. There are likely to be errors in any data entry procedures which are working from historical sources. Errors may occur whether data is entered manually or if sources are machine-read. However, there are techniques that may be employed to assist the data entry process and ensure that it is as accurate as possible. Some large projects which are using a series of data entry operators employ a system of transcribing the original source onto a template before entering the data into the computer. The Genealogical Society of Utah's project to enter the entire 1881 census for the United Kingdom utilised this approach. For this project the census data was transcribed, not once, but twice, and evaluated by a third independent operator. This procedure is, however, immensely time consuming. Smaller projects may wish to employ a system of transcription before data entry, particularly, if the sources are difficult to read. In this way, problematic words or values may be identified and resolved prior to data entry. Transcriptions from the source to a template may also speed up the data entry process as the operator will be reading off a typed form rather than an illegible manuscript. Scanners and digital cameras also aid in overcoming transcription difficulties. If the source material is captured as a digital image, software may be used to enhance, enlarge or 'clean-up' hitherto illegible manuscripts. The digitised images may also be attached to or embedded within the database in order to allow users access to the original source. There are copyright issues with capturing images from manuscript sources in this manner and many local record offices and archives forbid the practice or charge a fee. Once sources have been digitised, **optical character recognition** (OCR) software may be utilised to convert the image to text. Most OCR packages use artificial intelligence systems to 'train' the software to work with the source material provided. This is particularly important for historical material. Typewritten or typeset sources often have malformed or inconsistent letters. However, although OCR software is rapidly improving in accuracy, it is still difficult to find programs that will cope with early modern handwriting.

Many database programs have features to facilitate the data entry procedure. First, fields may be designated as 'required' which means that the program will not allow the column to be left blank when entering information. Second, a default value could be entered in the field. If the majority of entries in one column are the same, setting this item as the default value will save inputting the same data again and again. Third, some programs have an option to allow one of only two options to be entered such as Yes/No, True/False, Guilty/Not Guilty. A modification of this is to use a 'look-up' table which consists of a fixed list of values that may be entered into a particular field. Fourth, validation rules may be entered into the design of the database. These will forbid some transcription errors. For example, validation rules could be set to ensure that the data entered in a 'date of death' field was not earlier than the 'date of birth' field for the same person. Finally, most database software allows the automatic generation of unique numbers.

Database programs usually provide two alternative methods for data entry purposes. These are illustrated for a fictional crime database in Figure 4.3.

a. The data sheet

Offences					
Record number	Prisoner ID	Offence number	Offence	Offence code	Circumstance
1	1	1	Theft of a wooden lamp	th	Sentenced
2	2	1	Theft of a cast metal retort door	th	Sentenced
3	3	1	Theft of a cast metal retort door	th	Sentenced
4	4	1	Reckless driving	en	Sentenced
5	5	1	Assault	as	Sentenced
6	6	1	Theft of a silver watch	th	Sentenced
7	7	1	Theft of a bottle of whiskey	th	Sentenced

b. The form

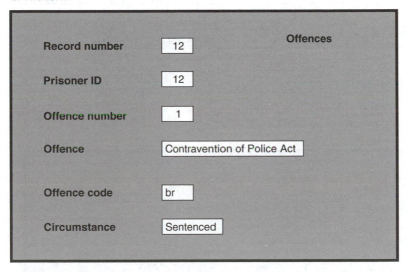

Figure 4.3 Data entry methods for single tables.

The data sheet method organises the database into a conventional tabular structure allowing information to be entered in columns and rows. The form method enables the user to design their own template for data entry purposes. Rather than viewing the whole table at once, the information is presented record by record. The form method is particularly useful where tables have many fields and therefore may not be viewed on one screen without scrolling backwards and forwards. Forms are also invaluable where data needs to be entered into more than one table. Here, the potential for errors is at its highest. The options are again illustrated using the crime database in Figure 4.4.

The alternatives are: to enter information into one table at a time – with this method there would need to be cross-checking from one table to another to ensure that the data is consistent across the different tables; to have two or more data sheets open side by side; or to design a form based on a number of tables to allow the information to be entered into more than one table at a time. Figure 4.4 demonstrates

a. The data sheets

			Offences		
Record number	Prisoner ID	Offence number	Offence	Offence code	Circumstance
1	1	1	Theft of a wooden lamp	th	Sentenced
2	2	1	Theft of a cast metal retort door	th	Sentenced
3	3	1	Theft of a cast metal retort door	th	Sentenced
4	4	1	Reckless driving	en	Sentenced
5	5	1	Assault	as	Sentenced
6	6	1	Theft of a silver watch	th	Sentenced
7	7	1	Theft of a bottle of whiskey	th	Sentenced

			Prisoners					
Record number	Prisoner ID	Admission year	Forename	Surname	Age	Gender	Marital status	Birthplace
1	1	1861	Jane	Henderson	28	f	m	Glasgow
2	2	1861	John	McCulloch	43	m	m	Oban
3	3	1861	Donald	McCulloch	31	m	m	Glasgow
4	4	1861	Edward	McDivott	25	m	u	Ireland
5	5	1861	James	Madden	21	m	u	Ireland
6	6	1861	James	Matheson	20	m	m	Glasgow
7	7	1861	Thomas	Sherridan	20	m	u	Ireland

b. A multi-table form

Figure 4.4 Data entry methods for more than one table.

the advantages of the form view. All the fields from both the Offences and Prisoners tables are portrayed on the form. However, the Record Number and Prisoner ID data only has to be entered once on the form, although the information will be added to both tables. This reduces the likelihood of errors.

As the crime database demonstrates, **coding** may be another strategy to speed up the process of data entry. In the Offences table, the offence field is coded. For example, 'th' is used in place of theft; 'en' for endangering lives; and 'as' for assault. The advantages of coding are that information may be standardised and that data entry may not be as time consuming. Coding may take two forms: pre-coding where all standardisation is undertaken before data-entry and post-coding where a coding scheme is tacked on to the database following data entry. There are problems with coding. It is essential to maintain an accurate code book, detailing the reasoning behind the coding scheme and listing the codes and their descriptors. This in itself is often a protracted process and may negate the benefits in terms of the time taken. There is also the issue of the database becoming further removed from the original source material. Therefore many historians include two fields, one containing the exact information from the source and a second giving the code. Occupational information is particularly susceptible to this approach to coding. It is important to include the rich variety of occupational titles contained in many historical sources. However, the sheer quantity of occupations listed in a database may make analysis difficult. For example, by listing the occupations of voters in eighteenth-century England, it is possible to see the wide variety of their economic and social backgrounds. However, arguing that all the ginger-beer manufacturers voted Tory, when there is only one in the source may not be as persuasive as stating that 80 per cent of professionals voted for the party. Occupational classification schemes may be specific to the project, coding occupations for a particular purpose. Alternatively historians may adopt one of the general occupational classification schemes developed by statisticians such as Charles Booth. Coding, particularly of occupational information, will be discussed in more detail on pages 99–101.

Another approach to encourage speed and accuracy in data entry, is to standardise the information in the source. In this process, dates, units of measurement and spelling variations are all normalised before data entry takes place. This is a controversial practice to many historians who argue that this form of pre-coding results in the final database being too far removed from the original source material. A decision made by one researcher to correct an 'error' in the source and standardise the information may prove contentious to another historian who views the 'error' as an interesting anomaly. However, some of these concerns could be alleviated if thorough documentation is prepared during the process of pre-coding which allows others to understand the judgements made on particular pieces of information. A form of standardisation that has been extensively debated by historians is the normalisation of nominal data to ease the process of linking names from different sources. Variant spellings of both forenames and surnames make record linkage on name fields particularly problematic. The issues and debates surrounding nominal record linkage will be further discussed (see pages 103–105).

During the data entry process, especial care should be taken to back up the database regularly. Many programs contain automatic systems to save data frequently, and these should be enabled. However, to guard against machine failure, loss, damage or theft the database should be backed up onto another medium, perhaps on a **flash memory stick, floppy disk, CD-ROM** or **zip drive**. If possible, copies should be kept in different locations. Although these precautions may seem excessive, the labour involved in these procedures should be measured against the work involved in re-creating the database from scratch if it was lost.

Once data entry has been completed a series of checking procedures should be undertaken. This process is known as **data cleaning**. As has been shown, some errors of data entry may be checked by transcription of the source prior to data entry or validation methods provided by the database software. However, this will not eliminate all data entry errors. The database should be proof read manually, usually from a hard copy. However, there are some mechanical processes that can aid this procedure. First, many programs have spell-checkers, which, although not infallible may identify some obvious errors. Second, the database should be queried to check the integrity of the data. For example, fields may be sorted which will indicate where the first character has been entered incorrectly. Alternatively, frequency counts will highlight other errors of transcription, for instance a frequency count on an occupation field will reveal typing errors such as *atorney* instead of attorney or *sevrant* in place of servant.

Querying the database

Once data entry and data cleaning processes have been completed, the database is ready for analysis. Different methods of querying and analysing data will be discussed shortly (see pages 88–94).

Data documentation

As has been apparent throughout this discussion of database creation, it is good practice to prepare thorough documentation throughout the process to support the computer-based database. This is particularly important if the database is to be used by people, other than the designers/creators, as what may seem self-evident to them, may be incomprehensible to an uninitiated user. In addition, if the database is to be deposited in a data archive such as the Arts and Humanities Data Service History section based at the University of Essex, full documentation will need to be provided. Archiving the data is to be encouraged. One of the main benefits of a machine-readable source is that it may be utilised by a wide range of researchers for many purposes, and certainly for objectives beyond those first envisaged by the designer and creator. Data archives will also ensure that the database will be preserved. In a world of rapidly changing software and hardware, it is important for electronic resources to be conserved against obsolescence. For this reason, it may be sensible to save the database, not only in the format provided by the database software, but also in **ASCII** format (a basic international standard of text representation). Most database programs will be able to import databases in this format, whereas they may not support other software packages.

The contents of the documentation should provide the following:

- detailed information on the source material used in the database with archival references and/or publication details;
- the aims and objectives of the original project which created the resource;
- database design decisions, such as number of tables, fields included or why certain formats were chosen;
- database creation issues including any codebooks or decisions about the standardisation of source material;
- if the source material was sampled and if so, how, and why;
- any problems encountered with the database design and creation.

The documentation will prove to be invaluable, not merely for the original research project but particularly if the database is to be used by others. Although it may seem excessive for a small project to create any documentation to accompany the database, much of this information may be contained within the database program itself and therefore negate the need for additional supporting material.

▶ Analysis and information retrieval

Once a database has been constructed or acquired as a machine-readable resource, it is ready to be analysed for the purposes of the research project. This section will outline some of the simple and more complex analyses that may be undertaken using most database packages.

Viewing

Although this operation may appear to be an obvious one, viewing data tables, either as forms or as data sheets is an imperative starting point for any researcher. This enables a comparison to be undertaken between the original source and the database. In addition, records may be located using the 'Find' or 'Go to record' tools provided with the database software. For those perhaps interested in tracing a particular family or name in a census database, the 'Find' tool may be sufficient for their purposes. Viewing the database also reveals the number of records it contains (or the total population) and the variety of fields.

Sorting

Sorting the database allows the user to view the table in a variety of different forms. By so doing, patterns begin to emerge which may suggest lines of enquiry that are worth pursuing. One of the most basic forms of sorting the database, is to organise names into alphabetical order. This process is most helpful in source material that is organised in other ways. For example, the order of the census was determined by the enumerator, and rent rolls are often organised in property order which makes it difficult to locate particular individuals. The census may also be sorted into alphabetical order of street names. This helps to reconstruct the town, village or parish, especially when streets cross enumeration districts or parish boundaries. Sorting just one field, if it is a field that contains numerous values which are exactly the same, such as street name, may not be sufficient. In these cases, it is important to sort the table by further fields. Table 4.3 demonstrates how this might operate for the 1861 census database of Beverley in Yorkshire. The table was sorted first by street name, then by house number, then by surname and finally by person ID number. Therefore Beckside, a street which ran across more than one enumeration district can be reconstructed by household. Sorting of alphabetical fields is usually performed in ascending order, that is from A to Z. However, when sorting numerical fields, it may be worthwhile to consider sorting in descending order, that is from the highest number to the lowest. This for example, would reveal the oldest person and their occupations in the census, or the person who paid the highest tax from a hearth tax record. Table 4.4 shows the Beverley census depicted in age order. Sorting the database is important to establish areas for further analysis. The Beverley example, for instance, confirms that the three oldest residents were women, but that the most elderly members of the workforce were both men.

Querying

Very simply, querying allows the researcher to select a subsection of the whole database. The querying, or filtering as it is referred to in some software packages, allows the user to choose which records or fields to view. If the master table is perceived as a set, when it is queried information will be filtered out into subsets. For example, all the servants from a census table, the male defendants found guilty of murder from an assize database, or farmers who voted Liberal from an elections dataset. In order to retrieve the information from the database a query language will be used.

Table 4.3 Beverley census of 1861 sorted by address, house number, surname and person ID

Person ID	House number	Address	First name	Surname	Condition	Age	Sex	Relation to head	Occupation	Birthplace
789	1	Beckside	John J.	Jackson	Married	27	M	Head	Joiner	Little Kelk, Yorkshire
790	1	Beckside	Elizabeth	Jackson	Married	25	F	Wife		Hull, Yorkshire
791	1	Beckside	Walter	Jackson	Unmarried	2	M	Son		Beverley, Yorkshire
792	1	Beckside	Frederick	Jackson	Unmarried	0.75	M	Son		Beverley, Yorkshire
793	2	Beckside	John	Fowler	Married	46	M	Head	Butcher	Cottingham, Yorkshire
794	2	Beckside	Harriet	Fowler	Married	46	F	Wife		Hull, Yorkshire
795	2	Beckside	Isabella	Thompson	Unmarried	18	F	Servant	House servant	Hull, Yorkshire
796	3	Beckside	Jane	Wilson	Unmarried	43	F	Head	Schoolmistress	Beverley, Yorkshire
797	3	Beckside	Hannah	Owen	Widowed	52	F	Sister	Mariner's wife	Bishop Burton, Yorkshire
798	3	Beckside	Sarah	Owen	Unmarried	14	F	Niece	Scholar	Beverley, Yorkshire
799	3	Beckside	John	Wilson	Unmarried	14	M	Son	Lawyer's clerk	Beverley, Yorkshire

Source: Beverley census database.

Table 4.4 Beverley census of 1861 sorted by age in descending order

Person ID	House number	Address	First name	Surname	Condition	Age	Sex	Relation to head	Occupation	Birthplace
738	105	Keldgate	Isabella	Maniland	Widowed	88	F	Mother-in-law	Labourer's wife	Newark, Nottinghamshire
539	62	Norwood	Catherine	Steel	Widowed	87	F	Head	Formerly laundress	Beverley, Yorkshire
709	99	Keldgate	Hannah	Hardcastle	Married	86	F	Wife		Beverley Parks, Yorkshire
93	28	Norwood Walk	James	Coventry	Widowed	84	M	Father	Gardener	Scotland
953	6	Holme Church Lane	James	Warters	Married	83	M	Head	Waterman	York, Yorkshire
871	28	Holme Church Lane	Ann	Binnington	Married	83	F	Wife		Aike, Yorkshire
1,104	44	Beckside	Thamar	Hodgson	Widowed	82	F	Head	Distiller's wife	Yapham, Yorkshire
870	28	Holme Church Lane	John	Binnington	Married	82	M	Head	Retired shoemaker	Sutton, Yorkshire
32	10	Norwood	Ann	Hunsley	Widowed	81	F	Head	Formerly Farmer's wife	Easingwold, Yorkshire
1,346	38	Grovehall	Emma	Collison	Widowed	81	F	Mother	Clerk in Custom's Hall's wife	Cranswick, Yorkshire
984	15	Beckside	Ann	Verity	Widowed	81	F	Head	Skinner's wife	Driffield, Yorkshire

Source: Beverley census database.

The standard format for query languages is **Structured Query Language** or SQL and most proprietary database programs are based on this format often with bespoke extensions to the basic language. SQL was designed by IBM in the 1970s and is an interactive language for recovering information from, defining and updating a database. Figure 4.5 illustrates an SQL- formatted query to find out all the individuals in the Beverley census who were aged over 50 and unmarried. However, most database programs, even though based on SQL allow a more intuitive form of querying called '**query by example**', and therefore it is no longer necessary for researchers to learn SQL in order to query their data.

A number of strategies may be employed to make effective use of queries:

* queries may be gradually extended or contracted by refining them;
* combining criteria for efficient searching;
* making full use of Boolean algebraic operators such as AND, OR, NOT;
* using wild card characters and indices for fuzzy matching.

Refining queries

One of the main advantages of employing computers to analyse source material, rather than searching documents manually, is the flexibility, efficiency and speed that automation allows. Refining queries is a process that permits the historian to discern patterns and outline further research possibilities. If the criteria in queries are defined too narrowly no records, or too few to make sense of the question may be returned. If the criteria are too inclusive, the number of records returned may make analysis unwieldy. For example, a researcher may wish to discover the number of servants in a particular population using the census. Therefore, they enter the **search string**, "servant" under the *Occupation* field. In the Beverley census of 1861 this returns three records – clearly an underestimation of the number of servants in the population. The query is then modified to select all those described as servants under the *Relation to Head* field. This recovers over 80 records and the occupational titles include: cooks, housekeepers, coachmen, kitchen maids, gardeners, governesses and grooms. However, in this example, the three earlier records were not returned, because the individuals concerned were denoted as boarders or visitors under the *Relation to head* field. It is clear, that any strategy to ascertain information on the number of servants in the population using the census as a source would need to take into account information from both the *Occupation* and *Relation to head* fields. It would also be essential not to define 'servant' in too limited a fashion, otherwise legitimate occupational titles could be excluded.

Combining criteria

Step-by-step querying as described above is an effective strategy because it allows the researcher to evaluate the records returned at each stage of the process. However, it is

a. Query

SELECT ALL WHERE age >50 AND status = "Unmarried"

b. Result

Person ID	House number	Address	First name	Surname	Condition	Age	Sex	Relation to head	Occupation	Birthplace
14	5	Hunsley's Yard	Thomas	Wilson	Unmarried	78	M	Head	Gentleman's servant	Etton, Yorkshire
109	33	Norwood Walk	Sarah	Marshall	Unmarried	63	F	Head	Formerly servant	Bridlington Quay, Yorkshire
110	33	Norwood Walk	Hannah	Lawson	Unmarried	78	F	Boarder	Annuitant	Stokesley, Yorkshire
302	3	Waltham Terrace	William	Wilson	Unmarried	55	M	Boarder	Agricultural labourer	Hull, Yorkshire
333	11	Waltham Terrace	Mary	Griffin	Unmarried	64	F	Head	Laundress	North Cliff, Yorkshire
374	20	Waltham Terrace	Bessy	Dyson	Unmarried	51	F	Sister-in-law	Laundress	Skidby, Yorkshire
503	51	Norwood	William	Piercy	Unmarried	61	M	Head	Retired farmer	Tibthorp, Yorkshire
637	83	Minstermoorgate	William	Foord	Unmarried	56	M	Boarder	Draper	Hull, Yorkshire
1,009	22	Beckside	Mary	Lightly	Unmarried	70	F	Head	Formerly monthly nurse	Hull, Yorkshire
1,382	84	Riding Fields	John	Carr	Unmarried	62	M	Head	Retired baker	Beverley, Yorkshire

Figure 4.5 An SQL query on the Beverley census.
Source: Beverley census database.

not the most effective way of searching and retrieving information from a database. The step-by-step approach is particularly useful in defining and refining queries that may be applied to a series of other sources. For example, the historian researching servants may refine the query using the Beverley enumeration books, but then apply the outcome of the process to a series of census registers for other locations. Combining search criteria is a more efficient method of retrieving information, but this more economic method may entail less understanding of the nuances of the source material. An analysis of women and crime using the assize records may be achieved by using a combined criteria strategy. For example, the number of female servants convicted of theft could be ascertained by entering "female" in the *Sex* field, "servant" in the *Occupation* field, theft in the *Offence* field, and "convicted" in the *Outcome* field.

Boolean operators

Boolean logic provides a further way to refine queries and to ask more complex questions of the source. The *AND* operator is employed to narrow the search criteria and may be used within one field or to combine a number of fields. For example, in an *Occupation* field the *AND* operator may be used to return all those working as bootmakers and shoemakers, grocers and drapers, or carpenters and joiners. Alternatively, the *AND* operator may be used to link information from a number of fields: perhaps married (*Status* field) women (*Sex* field) who were heads of households (*Relation to head* field) or children under the age of 15 (*Age* field) who were born in the county (*Birthplace* field). The *OR* operator is used to widen the search and return more records. The investigation into the crimes committed by female servants could be broadened to include 'theft or murder or assault' in the *Offence* field. The *NOT* operator is used to return records that do not meet the criteria specified. Using the *NOT* operator is often a more efficient method of searching a database. For example, a study of migration may wish to establish the number of individuals who were born in the community and the number who moved into the area from elsewhere. In the Beverley census this could be achieved by listing all the possible places of origin under the *Birthplace* field: Hull, Leeds, Lincoln, London, and so on. A more effective method is to enter NOT 'Beverley Yorkshire' instead. The *NOT* operator may also be used to return all records containing information in a particular field. Therefore entering NOT '**Null**' under an occupation field will return only the records which contain occupational titles. This is particularly useful for records where there may be many blank entries, for example married women's occupations in census registers or addresses of witnesses in legal records.

Fuzzy matching

Wildcard expressions are used by many computer programs and search engines to signify any character or characters. The most common wildcard expressions are '?' to signify a particular character and '*' to represent a series of characters. For example

"Sm?th" would return surnames spelt either Smith or Smyth; "b*r" would return occupations such as builder, butcher, book-keeper or bricklayer; "*smith" would assist those researching the metal trades by recovering any occupation ending in the word "smith" such as blacksmith, goldsmith, coachsmith or gunsmith; and "*theft*" would return any mention of the word theft in a list of offences.

Names in historical sources provide a particular challenge for the historian and researcher. Variant spelling of names was common until the nineteenth century. Many documents were compiled by scribes recording the information given to them verbally and what may be known as oral/aural confusion is widespread in many sources. For example, the name Oldfield may be recorded as Oldford, Aldfield or Aldford. This problem may be compounded by local dialects. There may also be transcription errors with letters accidentally transposed, omitted or replaced. Records composed contemporaneously and under pressure are particularly susceptible to this form of confusion. Therefore, in order to search or query surnames many database software packages incorporate a method of fuzzy matching based on how names sound as opposed to how they are spelt. The most famous of these is an index first developed by Robert Russell in 1918 known as **SOUNDEX**. A modified SOUNDEX index has been standardised by the National Archives and Records Administration in the United States. Surnames that sound the same, but are spelled differently, like SMITH and SMYTH, have the same code and therefore may be located even if recorded under various spellings. The SOUNDEX code consists of a letter and three numbers. The letter is always the first letter of the surname. The numbers are assigned to the remaining letters of the surname and zeroes are added at the end if necessary, to produce a four-character code. Additional letters are disregarded. Table 4.5 outlines the main rules for the SOUNDEX coding system. SOUNDEX is most appropriate for post-nineteenth-century records and names of Anglo-Saxon origin. Therefore, many historians have developed variations of the SOUNDEX code in order to address the vagaries of names in particular records. The Thame Local History Society in the United Kingdom for example, have produced their own four (occasionally five) letter initial surname code known as FISK to manage names in early modern English source material. The FISK is generated from the first letter of a surname plus three or four other consonants from the surname. Vowels are only used in the code when they occur as the first letter of the surname. A full stop is used if there is no second, third or fourth letter available. Surnames are grouped to include all possible variants, therefore Davies, Davis, Davidson and Davison are placed in the same cluster. Such indices may already have been incorporated into the database software for use in querying or may be added or modified.

Statistics

Many database software packages are now equipped with basic statistical functions. Thus, they will be able to perform some simple statistical operations on

Table 4.5   SOUNDEX coding rules

Number	Represents the letters
1	B, F, P, V
2	C, G, J, K, Q, S, X, Z
3	D, T
4	L
5	M, N
6	R

The letters A, E, I, O, U, H, W and Y are disregarded.

1. **Names with double letters**
   If the surname has any double letters, they should be treated as one letter.
2. **Names with letters side-by-side that have the same SOUNDEX code number**
   If the surname has different letters side-by-side that have the same number in the SOUNDEX coding guide, they should be treated as one letter. For example, Ja**cks**on or Schmi**dt**.
3. **Names with prefixes**
   If a surname has a prefix, such as Van or De it should be coded twice with and without the prefix because the surname might be listed under either code.
4. **Consonant separators**
   If a vowel (A, E, I, O, U) separates two consonants that have the same SOUNDEX code, the consonant to the right of the vowel is coded.

Source: 'Using the Census SOUNDEX', *General Information Leaflet 55* (Washington, DC: National Archives and Records Administration, 1995).

appropriate (numerical) data. These statistical functions usually include a calculator for the maximum and minimum values, the average, standard deviation and total. In addition, more complex arithmetical operations may be carried out by entering expressions. However, if it is necessary to perform more extensive statistical calculations the table should be exported to a spreadsheet or statistical analysis package. See Chapter 5 for details on historians' uses of spreadsheets.

Grouping

A further useful form of analysis, is to organise the information in the database into groups. This procedure may be carried out either by using the query or the report features of database programs. For example, the census register may be grouped by household, enabling researchers to assess the number or children or servants per household. Freemen's rolls, apprentice registers, or account books may be organised by year to discover the number of freemen and apprentices enrolled or the income and expenditure per year. Figure 4.6 charts the results of a query based on the Harbury census of 1881. The census was grouped under the head of household, and then the number of individuals within each household was counted.

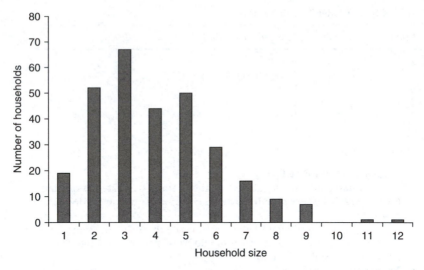

Figure 4.6   Grouping by size of household in Harbury, Warwickshire, 1881.
Source: Harbury census database.

The program requires a field which uniquely identifies each record on which to base the count. Therefore, frequency counts are usually performed on the field containing the desired values (e.g. *Occupation* or *Year*) and on the *ID* field.

Grouping procedures may also be carried out on one field. This process is known as a frequency count or sorting by frequency. The number of unique entries in one field are counted producing a summary of the values. Thus for example, the different types of occupations may be counted or the number of votes for a particular politician. The resulting information is often sorted into descending order illustrating the most numerous occupations in a town or the most popular political party. The results may also be converted to a chart for further emphasis. The frequency table in Table 4.6 shows the most common offences of prisoners from the database of Prosecutions for Violence in England, Australia and New Zealand. Frequency counts are useful tools to check for errors following data entry. Therefore, a listing of occupations by frequency would highlight any mistyping such as Acountant or Bker. Frequency tables may also be employed to post-code the information either by standardising entries or re-categorising them into groups for ease of analysis. For example, a frequency count of the *Birth place* field in the Beverley census database reveals that there are 294 distinct places of birth for Beverley citizens in 1861. However, a re-categorisation of places into counties makes the analysis of migration patterns more manageable. For further information on categorisation see pages 101–103 that follow.

A modification of the frequency count is a table which summarises the information from more than one field. These tables are commonly known as **cross-tabulations**.

Table 4.6   Frequency count of offences

Offence	Number of accused
Abusive/violent language	475
Actual bodily harm	13
Aggravated assault	324
Aggravated assault on female	6
Aggravated assault on wife	21
Assaulting police officer	1,031
Attempted indecent assault	21
Attempted murder	32
Attempted rape	27
Attempted suicide	159
Common assault	10,198
Fighting	999
Grievous bodily harm	71
Indecent assault	141
Jostling	76
Malicious cutting/wounding	129
Manslaughter	19
Murder	24
Persistent cruelty	76
Rape	33
Suicide	99
Threats	1,405

Source: Prosecutions for violence in England, Australia and New Zealand database.

Cross-tabulations enable comparisons to be made between two fields. For example, a cross-tabulation of the *Occupation* and *Vote* fields of an election database will reveal whether there is a relationship between economic status and political behaviour. Figure 4.7 portrays the results of a cross-tabulation query on the *Age range* and *Sex* fields in the Beverley census. Any two fields may be compared using cross-tabulation queries. However, if there are too many different values in the field, a categorisation should be undertaken first. Thus in Figure 4.7 the *Age* field was re-categorised into ranges before the cross-tabulation was performed.

Queries on more than one table

Queries may be performed on more than one table at once. In these cases, the relationship between the tables needs to be established in order for the query to function properly. Often these links will be on pre-established ID fields, see for example the relationships outlined in Figure 4.1. On other occasions, the links will

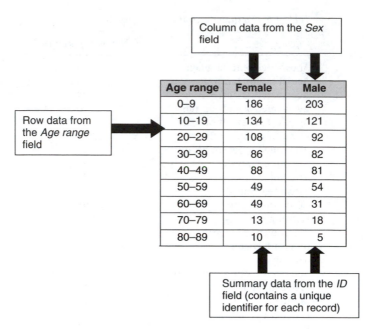

Age range	Female	Male
0–9	186	203
10–19	134	121
20–29	108	92
30–39	86	82
40–49	88	81
50–59	49	54
60–69	49	31
70–79	13	18
80–89	10	5

Column data from the *Sex* field

Row data from the *Age range* field

Summary data from the *ID* field (contains a unique identifier for each record)

Figure 4.7   Results of a cross-tabulation query on the Beverley census.
Source: Beverley census database.

be made between a field or fields in the tables. Figure 4.8 demonstrates such a linkage from the Halifax elections database. The links are made between the *First name, Surname, Address* and *Occupation* fields for the 1832 and 1835 poll books. Linking by name is a complex methodological issue and is discussed later (see pages 103–105). Queries may be undertaken on tables created from similar sources such as concurrent poll books; tables created from a variety of related sources such as tax records and parish registers; or tables created by the researcher to enhance the original source material such as occupational categorisation tables.

▶ Methodological issues

Throughout this discussion of the creation and analysis of historical databases, a number of methodological issues have been raised. Depending on the historical source that is being translated to a database, these procedural questions may need confronting at some stage of the project. There is no right or wrong approach but the methodology selected for particular problems should be fully explained in any accompanying text or documentation. For more information on these and other methodological problems facing users of historical databases see the **further**

a. Links between two tables from the Halifax elections database

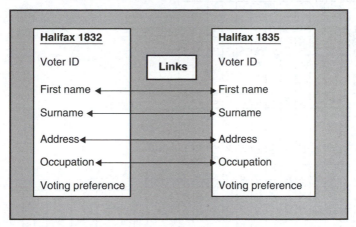

b. Result of a cross-tabulation query that compares voting preference in 1832 with voting preference in 1835

	1832 – Tory (%)	1832 – Liberal (%)	1832 – Split (%)	1832 – Did not vote (%)
1835 – Tory	83	2	8	7
1835 – Liberal	8	73	9	10
1835 – Split	57	20	12	11
1835 – Did not vote	3	4	31	62

Figure 4.8   Querying more than one table.

Source: West Riding elections database.

reading section. What follows is an overview of three of the key methodological areas that have faced historians using computerised databases

- Coding
- Occupational categorisation
- Nominal record linkage.

Coding

Coding used to be necessary because database management systems could not handle large amounts of text and fields were required to be of a fixed maximum width or number of characters. An example of a heavily coded database created in the 1980s is depicted in Figure 4.9.

These demands by software packages are no longer present but many historians still code their databases. They do so for three reasons: first, data entry may be

Table name = Coma										
ADMITTED MA	KEYCODE	NAME	DATCODE	MASUDAT	MALIDAT	MAINDAT	MASUCOL	MALICOL	MAINCOL
1500–19	1	MORWENT, ROBERT	503	A5110403	A5110618	A5110630	A16	A16	A16
1500–19	2	CLARKSON, RICHARD	506	A5130527	A5151211	A5160310	A08	A08	A08
1500–19	3	GARTH, JOHN	505	A5120423	A512	A5120704	A23	A23	A23
1520–29	4	WALSH, THOMAS	514	A5210617	A5210617	A5210709	A06	A06	A06
1500–19	8	HOLLE, ROBERT	514	A5210614	A5210617	A5170709	A06	A06	A06
1520–29	8	HOLLE, ROBERT	514	A5210614	A5210617	A5170709	A06	A06	A06
1500–19	9	LEE, GEOFFREY	517	A5100426	A5110618	A5110630	A16	A16	A16
1520–29	12	BARLOW, JOHN	513	A5201207	A5200705	A5290126	A18	A18	A18
1520–29	15	DENE, KENELM	515	A5220207	A5230210	A5230323	A06	A06	A06
1520–29	16	COREN, RICHARD	515	A5211115	A5230210	A5230323	A06	A06	A06
1520–29	18	GARRETT, THOMAS	514	A5230205	A5240309	A5240314	A16	A16	A16

Notes

Fields	Description	Code description
ADMITTED MA:	Date admitted to MA	Decade admitted
KEYCODE:	Student ID number	Unique identifier
NAME:	Student name	Full text
DATCODE:	Three figure date code	Year without century figure: 1512 = 512
MASUDAT:	MA supplication date	Year–Month–Day: A5110403 = 3rd April 1511
MALIDAT:	MA licentiate date	As above
MAINDAT:	MA inception date	As above
MASUCOL:	MA supplication college	College code: A06 = Corpus Christi
MALICOL:	MA licentiate college	As above
MAINCOL:	MA inception college	As above

Figure 4.9 Corpus Christi database demonstrating coding.

speeded up. This is particularly the case if simple codes are used. For example, 'M' for married, 'U' for unmarried and 'W' for widowed. However, the introduction of a complicated coding system may actually slow data inputting down whilst the data enterer checks terms in the code book. Second, because coding is a form of close assessment of the data and may lead to the development of categories for ease of analysis (see 'Occupational categorisation' later). Third, coding may facilitate the process of record linkage – particularly nominal record linkage (see later).

The decision to code need not be taken before the creation of the database unless it is to smooth the process of data entry. For data entry purposes, the field being pre-coded should not contain too many different pieces of data. For example, it is not difficult to code a field with 'M' representing male and 'F' representing female but coding 150 different occupations or places of residence may be more problematic. This is particularly the case if a robust coding scheme is not established at the outset. If the person entering data encounters a rogue piece of information, it would be frustrating to re-design the whole coding scheme.

If the data is being post-coded then the use of a hierarchical coding scheme is suitable for many types of data. For example, the 1851 census organised occupations first into twelve classes and then into sub-classes for each group. Geographical data may be similarly organised into parishes, counties, countries and continents or using numbers of miles or kilometres from a focal point. For other data, a substitution system may be used, exchanging a simplified or standardised version of a word or words for the more complex and numerous variations. Some historians prefer using numbers rather than letters or abbreviations for their coding scheme (see Figure 4.9). Numbers have the advantage of being quick to enter – however, beware: the scope for data entry errors is exceptionally high.

Any coding scheme should make decisions in the light of other classification systems used by historians. This will enable full comparisons to be made between similar pieces of research. Alternative coding systems may also be used on one set of data, perhaps refining categorisations used in other related literature.

Finally, a full code book should be developed to form part of the documentation to accompany the database. The code book should provide a short introduction detailing how the decisions to code particular items were made, followed by a detailed description of the coding scheme.

Occupational categorisation

A particular use of post-coding is to sort information in particular fields into classes or categories. This is important to assist in analysis where the numbers of unique values in a field are especially numerous. One of the most common types of classification is the categorisation of occupational information. A variety of organisational plans may be used, but the chief objectives of any scheme are: to produce an occupational analysis commensurate with other research in the field; and to provide as complete a picture as possible regarding the status and occupation of the population under consideration. For modern historians a number of standardised occupational classifications exist, for example those designed to accompany the decennial censuses from the early nineteenth century and later modified by Charles Booth for his survey of London. For those using earlier records, it may be necessary to devise an individual scheme.

As an example of the difficulties historians face, consider the categorisation of the occupations of voters in nineteenth-century elections in Table 4.7.

There are slight, but significant differences between the various approaches to the problem of occupational categorisation. Nossiter's use of a drink category is logical (the drinks trade was very influential in Victorian elections) but few other analysts have followed his example. Morris uses an innovative approach looking at the products being produced and the organisation of work but few other electoral historians have followed his lead. A compromise is to use a multi-dimensional approach. In this method each occupation is classified using several different strategies. For example,

Table 4.7   A comparison of voters' different occupational categorisation schemes

Morris (organisation)	Morris (production)	Nossiter	O'Gorman	Phillips
Agriculture	Food	Gentlemen and professionals	Gentlemen and professionals	Gentlemen and professionals
Quarry	Milk	Manufacturers and merchants	Merchants and manufacturers	Merchants and entrepreneurs
Distribution and processing	Drink	Retail trade	Retailers	Retailers
Transport	Stone	Craft trade	Skilled craftsmen	Craftsmen/artisans
Commerce	Coal	Farming	Semi/unskilled labourers	Skilled workmen
Manufacturing	Metals	Drink	Agriculturalists	Labourers
Craft	Textiles	Other		Agriculturalists
Professional	Ropes			
Services	Chemicals			
Domestic	Glass			
Non-specific	Pottery Leather Timber Paper			

Source: R. J. Morris, 'Property titles and the use of British urban poll books', *Urban History Yearbook* (1983); T. J. Nossiter, *Influence, Opinion and Political Idioms in Reformed England* (Brighton, 1975); F. O'Gorman, *Voters, Patrons and Parties: The Unreformed Electoral System of Hanoverian England, 1734–1832* (Oxford, 1989); J. A. Phillips, *Electoral Behavior in Unreformed England, 1761–1802* (Princeton, 1982).

separating out the 'industrial' from the 'non-industrial' and giving a rudimentary 'social' as opposed to 'economic' ranking. Occasionally even individual occupational titles may be isolated where any categorisation would destroy the nuances of voters' work experiences. This approach ensures that comparisons may be made with other researchers and also that particular lines of inquiry suggested by the specific charac-teristics of the voting population under consideration may be analysed, without hav-ing to be constrained in a 'categoriser's strait-jacket'. The multi-dimensional design gives the analyst flexibility whilst allowing meaningful analyses to be undertaken.

Nominal record linkage

Nominal record linkage concerns all historians using data containing names. For example, in a prosopographical study the researcher has to determine (usually by context) that all the sources relate to the same person and not another person with the same name. For large quantities of nominal data such as parish registers, poll books and tax records computerised record linkage offers an efficient means of tracing individuals through different sources and across time periods. Modern data-bases processing large quantities of nominal data, for example censuses, use record linkage techniques to check accuracy levels.

There are two principal problems that have to be faced when adopting a computerised approach to record linkage:

- The existence of multiple common names. For example, the computer will link the first occurrence of 'David Jones' in one list with the first occurrence of 'David Jones' in other lists. Other supporting information however, may indicate that the two David Jones may not be the same person. This problem is particularly acute in local community studies where certain surnames are dominant. Jones is a particularly common surname in Wales for example, where a third of the community may have the same surname.
- The question of variation in spelling. For example, is a 'Robert Cooke esq.' in one list the same as a 'Bob Cook' in another list?

Historians therefore devise and apply a system of rules to assist in the process of record linkage. These rules employ other supporting information to supplement the nominal data. Therefore, you may be more certain that the two David Jones should be linked as the same individual if they were also both butchers and lived at number 3, the High Street. Rules for automated record linkage are often best applied to detailed demographic data. It makes sense, for example, to specify that an individual's birth must precede his death or that the mother of a child should be more than 15.

Data structured more simply, such as trade directories or poll books, pose more dif-ficult record linkage problems and the possibility of making false links is higher than in complex data such as census material. Nominal record linkage is, however, easier with people of higher status and those who are geographically stable. Therefore, as the electorate were an elite in eighteenth- and nineteenth-century British society, it is easier to identify voters in the historical record than it is to distinguish vagrants.

Before any rules for record linkage are applied, the first step is to standardise (or code) the data contained within the historical source. This includes both names and other information such as occupations or place names. The coding of names may use the SOUNDEX system or an adaptation such as the FISK scheme used by the Thame Local History group. When coding surnames, a knowledge of local dialect may also be important. In a study of Cheshire poll books by Peter Adman, Stephen Baskerville and Katharine Beedham it was found that the endings '-del', '-dich', '-dil', '-dilch', '-eth', '-ith', '-tage', '-tedge' and '-tich' were all used interchangeably. It is important that every record in the database is unique. If there are two (or more) records that are exactly the same they should be discarded. Any linkage scheme should also avoid using information that relates to the behaviour and/or characteristics that are the objectives of the study. Thus an analysis of voting behaviour should avoid using voting preferences in the linkage process. Similarly a study of occupations should not use occupational data in the linkage exercise.

The system used may be fully-automated: that is where, once data is standardised, the computer makes all the decisions about linking records; or semi-automated, where the machine and the historian work together. The rules for record linkage systems usually start by trying to link names where every piece of supporting information in one source may be perfectly matched to information in the second source. For example, a linkage exercise using poll books may match individuals where the first name, surname, address and occupation are the same in each source. Those individuals whose data matches precisely are then removed from the database and placed in a separate file. The linkage process is then carried out again, this time using a less stringent list of matching information (perhaps just first name, surname and address). Each time the procedure is performed, the matching records are removed and checked, until finally all that remains are the records that could not be matched using the computer. Even then, a manual check should be done as rogue spellings or the use of a house name instead of a street name may result in a link which could not have been achieved by an automated process. This technique is known as a 'semi-automated, multiple pass system'. That is, a combination of computer and historian is used and the record linkage process is repeated several times using different pieces of information supporting the nominal data. As an illustration, the steps involved in linking two Halifax poll books of 1835 and 1837 are outlined in Table 4.8.

At each stage the two poll books were compared automatically by the software, using the specified fields. The resulting matches were then checked manually for accuracy and saved in a separate file. The subsequent passes through the two poll

Table 4.8   Nominal record linkage in practice

Steps	Number of records linked	Fields used for linkage
First pass	199	Surname, first name, address, occupation
Second pass	81	Surname, first name, occupation
Third pass	100	Surname, first name, address
Fourth pass	60	Surname, first name, occupation (standardised)
Fifth pass	26	Surname, first name, address (standardised)
Sixth pass	4	Manual check
Total	450	

Source: West Riding elections database.

books were carried out on those records which remained unmatched. Successfully connected records were added to the file containing the true links. Finally, a manual check of the remaining records in the two poll books was carried out in order to obtain a match for particularly difficult records. In the example three-quarters of the records that could be potentially linked (the number in the 1835 poll book) were successfully matched. A fully-automated system is often used for very large databases where the system of manual checks would be too time-consuming and not yield a statistically significant number of results.

▶ Further study

Recent advances in the analysis and dissemination of databases include the use of **Extensible Mark-up Language** (XML) as a method of querying more complex sources, and the transfer of databases onto the World Wide Web.

XML, the mark-up language developed for data transfer on the internet, has been used with complex historical sources such as probate inventories which do not translate easily into the regular structure of relational database models. The advantage of XML is that it does not impose a rigid structure upon the source and may be continually adapted for particular queries. The chief disadvantage is that as with any tagging or mark-up system the preparation and coding of the data takes considerably longer than fitting information into a simple data table. Therefore, it is unlikely that XML will offer an alternative to most researchers using databases but it will offer an opportunity to query data that will not easily fit the relational model. For more information on XML see Chapter 6.

Most modern database management systems have an option to allow the transfer of databases to the Web to allow external users to view and even to analyse data in a read-only format. The Web pages are usually formatted in **Dynamic Hyper Text Mark-up Language** (DHTML) which allows the database to run in its own window without any of the usual restrictions applied to Web pages by browsers although other formats are also available. This allows other users to interrogate the database dynamically via the Web and will form an important part of any dissemination strategy.

▶ Guide to further reading

Harvey, C. and Press, J., *Databases in Historical Research* (Basingstoke, 1996).

Thaller, M., *KLEIO. A Database System* (St. Katharinen, 1993).

Weatherill, L. and Hemingway, V., *Using and Designing Databases for Academic Work. A Practical Guide* (Newcastle, 1994).

Woollard, M. and Denley, P. (eds), *The Sorcerers's Apprentice. KLEIO Case Studies* (St. Katharinen, 1996).

5 Spreadsheets and the Historian

This chapter discusses the wide range of facilities offered by spreadsheet programs and their use by historians. From simple calculations to data analysis and presentation, the spreadsheet is an important multi-purpose tool for the historian. Spreadsheets serve as an entry point for the creation of simple databases, the employment of quantitative methods and the use of statistical operations to begin to interrogate historical sources.

▶ What is a spreadsheet?

Spreadsheets were introduced in 1978 as business software although they have since been adapted for a wide range of users. However, quantitative historical analysis began considerably earlier using statistical programs such as SPSS and SAS that were readily available from the late 1960s. These statistical packages will be briefly discussed at the end of the chapter. The name spreadsheet comes from accountants' spreadsheets, in which numbers, text or formulae to perform calculations are displayed in rows and columns. Spreadsheet software emulates the accountants' paper version usually presenting a screen with rows and columns and a space to enter formulae (see Figure 5.1). Conventionally, the columns are labelled with letters: A, B, C and so on and the rows are labelled with numbers: 1, 2, 3 … Each intersection of a column and a row is called a **cell** and identified using the letter/number reference, for example, A4, J138 or HH13. This reference is known as the **cell address**. Groups or ranges of cells may also need to be identified. A row of cells may be distinguished as B2:G2 that is, the cells B2, C2, D2, E2, F2 and G2. A column of cells could be described as H8:H16 and a block of cells by the range Q1:Z10. The **active cell** is the term for the cell currently being worked upon. Each file may have a number of spreadsheets contained within it. This is particularly useful for the historian who may wish to have a separate sheet for each census year or individual sheets for the data, for tables, and for graphs and charts.

Spreadsheets have a multiple of uses for the historian. Their main advantage for the business community is that data may be added and calculations are automatically amended across the entire spreadsheet. Therefore they are particularly

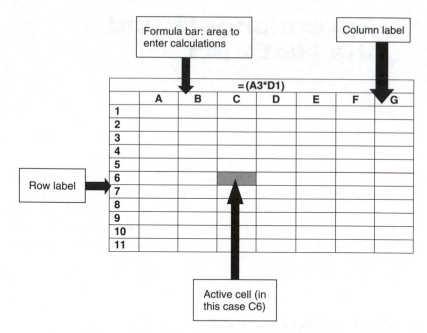

Figure 5.1   A blank spreadsheet.

appropriate for **dynamic** sets of information, that is data that is continually changing and being updated. At first sight then, the spreadsheet's main purpose may not appear to offer any great advantages to the historian. Historians' data is not normally dynamic having been collected in the past and it does not usually change once it has been entered into a program. However, it is the flexibility of the spreadsheet program that is of benefit to the practical work of the historian. The main functions of spreadsheet programs of use to historians are:

- To perform calculations and statistical operations on historical data;
- To act as a simple database program;
- To present information in a table, graph or chart.

▶ Calculations and statistics

The most obvious use of spreadsheets is to replicate their purpose for the business user with historical data. Many historical sources contain numbers: account books, price lists, wage books, court fines, subscriptions, and so on. A spreadsheet provides the most direct form of analysis for this quantitative data. Figures 5.2 and 5.3 give

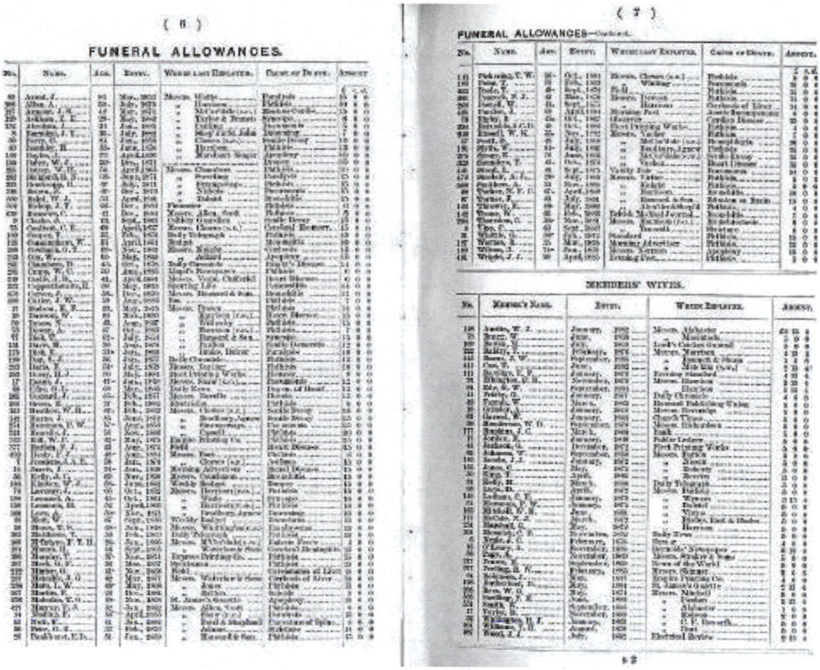
(6)

FUNERAL ALLOWANCES.

(7)

FUNERAL ALLOWANCES—Continued.

MEMBERS' WIVES.

Figure 5.2 A page of the London Society of Compositors account book, 1890.
Source: London Society of Compositors, 1890.

an example of such data from the London Society of Compositors, a trade union established in 1848. The list of funeral allowances supplies a rich source of information on the health hazards of working in the nineteenth-century printing industry, but also allows calculations to be performed to find out the average allowance given for funerals in different periods.

The translation of the original source to the spreadsheet immediately raises some questions. Note that the surname and first name have been entered in separate columns as have the month and year of entry into the register and the funeral allowance awarded. These decisions have been taken for ease of data analysis. For more information on the subject of data modelling and data entry, see Chapter 4. As with database programs, spreadsheets allow data to be described in a variety of formats according to the type of information entered. Table 5.1 explains the data types mainly used with historical data.

It is important that the data in each column is correctly described. It will not be possible for instance to perform calculations on data entered as 'Text' even if it contains only numbers. Once the data has been entered satisfactorily, it is possible to

	A	B	C	D	E	F	G	H	I	J	K
1	Number	Surname	First name	Age	Entry month	Entry year	Where last employed	Cause of death	Amount (l)	Amount (s)	Amount (d)
2	83	Avent	J.	84	March	1853	Messrs. Watts	Paralysis	15	0	0
3	108	Allan	A.	30	July	1879	Messrs. Harrison	Phthisis	10	0	0
4	127	Armour	J. S.	42	May	1874	Messrs. McCor'dale (s.r.)	Morbus Cordis	15	0	0
5	129	Askham	E. E.	29	May	1882	Messrs. Taylor & Francis	Syncope	8	0	0
6	152	Absolom	J.	21	January	1885	Messrs. Darling	Pneumonia	5	0	0
7	8	Burridge	J. Y.	36	July	1882	Messrs. Shep'd & St John	Drowning	7	0	0
8	39	Berry	C.	81	January	1850	Messrs. Clowes (s.r.)	Senile Decay	10	0	0
9	69	Boothby	H.	33	June	1876	Messrs. Harrison	Phthisis	13	0	0

Figure 5.3 The London Compositors spreadsheet.

Source: London Society of Compositors, 1890.

Table 5.1   Common spreadsheet data types for historical sources

General	No specific format
Numbers	For all numbers. The number of decimal places required may be specified and numbers may be displayed with or without a separator for the 1000s. Negative numbers may be displayed in red so that they stand out.
Currency	Allows currencies to be displayed with an appropriate monetary symbol (£, $, €, d̲, etc) and with two decimal places. Negative amounts may appear in red. Modern currencies only are catered for.
Date/time	Allows a variety of formats for displaying times and dates.
Percentage	Numbers entered here are multiplied by one hundred and displayed with a percentage sign.
Fractions	Displays data entered as fractions.
Text	Information entered in cells formatted as text is always treated as text even if numbers are included.

begin to use the information to perform calculations and statistical operations in order to enrich the analysis of the source. Most up-to-date spreadsheet programs now allow sophisticated statistical, financial and arithmetical analyses of information. However, this chapter will introduce only the most basic concepts, namely:

- summarising and describing data;
- relationships between data;
- dealing with series of data.

Summarising and describing data

The most common arithmetical and statistical operations summarise a series of numbers in a variety of ways to allow comparisons to be made with other information. At its most basic, this may be finding totals (sums) or subtotals of a series of figures. The London Society of Compositors data demonstrates one of the immediate problems historians have to face when performing even these most simple operations. In order to summarise the total expenditure of the union on funeral allowances, the amounts given in pounds, shillings and pence first need either to be converted to old pence or to be fully changed to decimal currency. This is because modern spreadsheet packages are unable to perform calculations on the old system of English currency (see Chapter 4, p. 80). To do this, the figures in the pounds column need to be multiplied by 240 (the number of old pence in the pound), and in the shillings column to be multiplied by 12 (the number of old pence in a shilling). The three columns are then added together and divided by 240 to come to an amount in decimal currency. Figure 5.4 demonstrates this process using the London

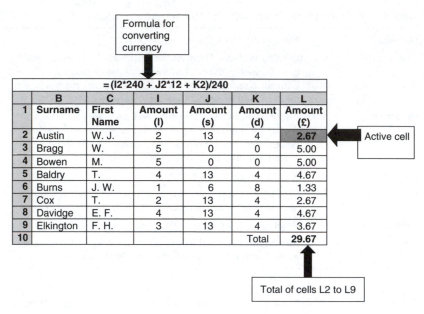

Formula for converting currency

= (I2*240 + J2*12 + K2)/240

1	B Surname	C First Name	I Amount (l)	J Amount (s)	K Amount (d)	L Amount (£)
2	Austin	W. J.	2	13	4	2.67
3	Bragg	W.	5	0	0	5.00
4	Bowen	M.	5	0	0	5.00
5	Baldry	T.	4	13	4	4.67
6	Burns	J. W.	1	6	8	1.33
7	Cox	T.	2	13	4	2.67
8	Davidge	E. F.	4	13	4	4.67
9	Elkington	F. H.	3	13	4	3.67
10					Total	29.67

Active cell

Total of cells L2 to L9

Figure 5.4 Converting currency.
Source: London Society of Compositors, 1890.

Society of Compositors dataset. The figures in column L have been rounded to two decimal figures which means that the total given in cell L10 does not quite accord with the figures displayed. Instead it gives the total amount of the raw figures not the rounded ones. Sources using other older forms of currency may also need to employ this process of conversion.

Other useful summaries include:

- Counting the number of items in a list. The **count** may involve counting *all* the items or just the unique ones;
- Finding the **maximum** and **minimum** values;
- The **range** of values, that is the difference between the highest and lowest values.

Spreadsheets also allow figures to be added together, subtracted, multiplied or divided. If any new information is included or removed the re-calculations will be carried out automatically.

For many historians finding the centre point of the range of values under consideration is an important part of summarising the data. This centre point or 'measure of central tendency' is often referred to as finding the **average** value.

There are three methods of calculating the average that are normally used:

- the **mean** or the arithmetic mean,
- the **median**,
- the **mode**.

When the term average is used, what is commonly meant is the arithmetic mean, although all three terms are different ways of calculating the average of a series of data. The mean is calculated by totalling the values under consideration and then dividing by the number of values. The disadvantage of using the mean alone is that if there are atypically large or small values included in the range of observations the mean will be distorted. The median is the value that lies in the middle of a ranked list of observations. Therefore if there is a list of thirteen items ranked in numerical order, the median value will be the seventh item on the list. There will be six items above and six below this value. If the list of items is an even number, then the median will be the average of the two middle values. If there are extreme atypical values the median will give a better interpretation of the central tendency than the mean. Finally, the mode is the most common of a set of observations. There may be more than one mode, producing a bi-modal or tri-modal distribution. The mode is of limited use if the values are very dispersed. Table 5.2 gives the mean, median and mode of the number of days prisoners were sentenced to in the Prosecutions for Violence database.

If the mean, median and mode lie close together, it means that the spread of values follows a **normal distribution**, that is one in a symmetrical, bell-shaped pattern. However, note that this bell-shape may not be apparent if there are very few values. Therefore, the number of large values is roughly the same as the number of small values. If the mode, median and mean diverge, the distribution will be asymmetrical or skewed, either to the upper or lower end of the range of values. With the sentences in the Prosecutions for Violence database it is clear that the spread of observations is a normal distribution. The mean, mode and median all give the measure of central tendency as a 29-day sentence. In distributions where most observations occur below the mean the distribution is described as **positively skewed**. For example, an analysis of family size in a community where the mean family size was 4.4 but there were a large number of 1, 2 or 3 member households and a lesser number of 10, 11 and 12 member households would produce a positively skewed distribution. Where most observations occur above the mean the distribution is described as **negatively skewed**. This might occur in an analysis of retirement ages where most individuals retired between the ages of 60 and 70 but there were a few individuals retiring early. In these cases, it is important to utilise all three measures of central tendency to describe the range of data fully.

A further factor may be introduced to assist in the description of the data. This is the measure of dispersion of the range of observations. At its most basic,

Table 5.2 Measures of central tendency using the Prosecutions for Violence database

Length of sentence (days)	Number of prisoners	Total length of sentence (days)
6	3	18
7	30	210
9	659	5,931
10	111	1,110
13	304	3,952
14	828	11,592
18	2	36
20	107	2,140
29	994	28,826
30	465	13,950
41	6	246
42	448	18,816
60	388	23,280
90	151	13,590
120	10	1,200
150	2	300
180	51	9,180
365	5	1,825
Total	4,564	136,202

Mean: Total length of sentence (1,36,202) divided by the total number of prisoners (4,564) = 136,202 ÷ 4,564 = **29.84 days.**

Mode: Most common value. The most (994) prisoners were sentenced to **29 days.**

Median: The middle value. The middle value occurs between the 2,282nd and 2,283rd values which again falls in the category of **29 days.**

Standard Deviation: The level of dispersion of a set of values. The standard deviation is **27.46 days.**

Source: Prosecutions for Violence in England, Australia and New Zealand database.

this measure of dispersion takes the form of the range: the lowest value subtracted from the highest. In the case of the Prosecutions for Violence database the range is 299 days (365 days − 6 days). The enormity of this range is an indication that the sentencing information may not fall into a normal distribution. The range also may be affected if the highest and lowest values are exceptionally large or small. The variability of the distribution may also be measured by considering the difference between two percentiles, usually the 25th and the 75th percentiles. The

25th percentile is the value in a range of values where 25 per cent of the measurements are less than or equal to it. The 25th and the 75th percentiles are usually called the lower and upper quartiles, respectively. A more sophisticated measure of dispersion is the **standard deviation** which calculates the amount of dispersion around the mean. Like the mean, the standard deviation takes into account *all* the values, not merely the extreme ones. However, it suffers from the same problem as the mean if the distribution is not a bell-shaped one.

Relationships between data

The summaries discussed above have related to one set of observations, data or variables. A **variable** is a measurable characteristic. It may be common to several sources or events and the value of the variable may change with each observation. In historical databases the variable usually equates to the field, therefore in the Prosecutions for Violence database, one variable is the length of the sentence. The value of the variable changes from prisoner to prisoner. Historians are often concerned with the relationships between two variables: for example, is there a connection between food shortages and political disturbances or are those living in rural areas more likely to have a conservative outlook? Statistical analysis allows the strength of the relationship between two variables to be measured precisely. The statistical analysis will measure the strength of any relationship – however absurd it may be. Therefore, the statistics may record a strong probability of a relationship between owning a goldfish and early age of marriage but this may not demonstrate an actual association. The first task of the historian is to investigate the reasons why two independent variables might be related. Only once these have been established should the relationship be measured using statistical techniques. The most common method of measuring the connection or **correlation** between two variables is to apply the **coefficient of correlation** to the two sets of data. The usual measure is Pearson's coefficient of correlation named after Karl Pearson who developed it, although this only measures the strength of a linear relationship. If the two sets of variables increase or decrease proportionately and simultaneously, the phenomena are **positively correlated**. If one variable increases in the same proportion that the other decreases, they are **negatively correlated**. The algorithm applied to the data to measure the correlation uses the level of deviation from the mean of each variable and the number of cases observed. A perfect positive correlation between two variables will result in a coefficient of +1. A perfect negative correlation will give a coefficient of −1. If there is no correlation the coefficient of correlation will be 0. It is rare for a correlation coefficient to be +1 or −1, particularly using historical data. It is far more likely that the coefficient of correlation returned by the spreadsheet will be in the range −0.7 to +0.7. Table 5.3 considers whether social class affected voting behaviour in some fictional UK constituencies.

Table 5.3 Are 'working-class' constituencies
more likely to vote Labour?

Voted Labour (%)	Working class (%)
17.6	41.8
53.6	67.3
10.4	23.7
11.6	36.6
29.6	51.7
49.6	49.4
62.4	55.3

Pearson's coefficient of correlation = +0.84.

The percentage of Labour voters in a constituency is considered alongside the percentage of those regarded as working-class. The Pearson coefficient of correlation returned is 0.84: a strong positive correlation. It is important when comparing variables that conclusions about individual behaviour are not automatically inferred from aggregate statistics. The most famous example of this so-called 'ecological fallacy' is when Emile Durkheim postulated that because suicide rates were higher in countries that were predominantly Protestant, Protestants were more likely to commit suicide than Catholics. In fact the countries he studied had many other differences besides their religious complexions. Moreover, he was using suicide rates for geographical areas not the numbers of suicides broken down by religious persuasion. Such studies may provide useful clues about relationships between different factors but conclusions about individuals are often only weakly supported by data on groups. There are statistical techniques to circumvent the problem of separating out individual behaviour from group behaviour. The most common technique is called ecological regression. However, these techniques have also been criticised for making assumptions about patterns of behaviour and using reductionism implying that groups act in a homogenised way.

Series of data

Another benefit of spreadsheets is that they are well-suited to analyse **time-series** data. That is, information that is collected chronologically over time. This could include information on wages, prices, imports and exports or levels of violent crime or illegitimacy. Figure 5.5 depicts typical time-series data, charting the number of baptisms and burials in the parish of Ashton, Lancashire from 1600 to 1650. Parish registers are useful sources for a consideration of demographic trends over time. However, a number of factors should be kept in mind when compiling information from the registers. There is often under-registration: predominantly at the change over from one vicar to another and in periods of crisis such as epidemic disease or

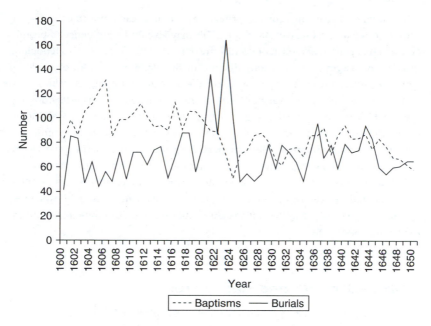

Figure 5.5   Time-series of baptisms and burials in the parish of Ashton, Lancashire 1600–50.

Source: Parish register data.

civil war; in periods of rapid population growth – by the early nineteenth century it is estimated that around a third of all births and deaths did not appear in the registers, and in areas where non-conformism was prevalent. Not all births were registered, particularly when there was a short period between birth and death and where babies were not baptised. Not all deaths may be registered in periods of plague or other epidemics, especially if the parish clerk and the vicar were among those affected.

Charting time-series data is a good starting point to identify particular trends or areas for investigation. The general trend in Figure 5.5 is of a decrease in the number of registered baptisms over time. In addition, the sharp increase in the number of burials in the years between 1620 and 1625 may indicate particular crises or epidemics which could be followed up in other sources.

Trend lines may be added to the chart in order to get a more accurate impression of the rate of growth over time. Trend lines take into account all the observations not just the first and last value in a series. Trend lines have also been used by historians to predict values for later time periods. **However this technique should only be used with extreme caution.** For example, the downward trend of baptisms in Lancashire in the seventeenth century does not take into account forthcoming industrialisation or the fact that records did not always detail the births of nonconformist or Catholic children.

By charting the data at regular intervals – for example each month or year – an extreme or atypical value will stand out. This may give undue influence or prominence to that particular month or year in the trend line. To overcome this tendency **moving averages** are used to smooth out the fluctuations in a chart over a long period of time. Moving averages calculate the average of a group of values over a period of time. The interval most commonly employed is a five-year moving average. Moving averages will also guard against data influenced by cyclical fluctuations. In these cases, it is important to analyse the data carefully to determine the periodicity of the cycle and to select the beginning and end years of the cycle. Often a five-year moving average may not be appropriate and a four-year, seven-year or nine-year moving average may be used instead. If an incorrect cycle is chosen, then the trend produced can be misleading. Figures 5.6 and 5.7 demonstrate how a five-year moving average smoothes out the fluctuations in the death rate in Ashton in the period 1600–1700.

▶ Spreadsheets and databases

Spreadsheet programs may be effectively employed in place of database management systems. The advantages of using a spreadsheet in place of a database program are:

- spreadsheets are simpler to use than most database programs;
- calculations and statistical operations may be carried out directly on the data;
- the presentation elements associated with spreadsheets are more extensive and easier to use than those associated with database programs;
- databases in spreadsheets are easily exported to database programs if more sophisticated data analysis is needed.

The disadvantages of using a spreadsheet program as a database include:

- spreadsheets only allow data to be represented as single table databases, so the relational functions are not available;
- the more advanced data analysis and querying functions are not present;
- the range of field types is not as extensive or as flexible;
- spreadsheets do not have true records only rows, this results in problems for managing records and builds in inflexibility.

Spreadsheets are therefore predominantly used by historians for projects with data that will easily fit the single file model; those which require calculations and statistical analyses; and/or at the end of projects to access the charting and graphing functions of the software. However, note that quantitative projects are not

Year	Burials	5-year moving average
1600	41	
1601	85	
1602	83	64.0
1603	47	64.6
1604	64	58.8
1605	44	51.8
1606	56	56.8
1607	48	54.0
1608	72	59.6
1609	50	62.8
1610	72	65.6
1611	72	66.0
1612	62	71.4
1613	74	67.2
1614	77	66.4
1615	51	71.6
1616	68	74.4
1617	88	70.2
1618	88	75.4
1619	56	89.0
1620	77	88.8
1621	136	104.2
1622	87	113.0
1623	165	107.2
1624	100	91.0
1625	48	83.4
1626	55	61.2
1627	49	56.8
1628	54	59.0
1629	78	
1630	59	

Note the smoothing out of the numbers of burials by using the moving average

Figure 5.6   The number of burials and the 5-year moving average of burials for Ashton, 1600–30.

Source: Parish register data.

necessarily small scale. The US Census Bureau, for example, has recently put some very large datasets, the tables from Historical Statistics of the United States, on its website [http://www2.census.gov/prod2/statcomp/index.htm].

When designing and creating a database for a spreadsheet the same planning and organisational steps outlined in Chapter 4 should be carried out. As the spreadsheet work area does not function as a database but merely as a series of columns, the identification of fields and field types is done one by one rather than looking at the whole. Therefore, it is very important to ensure that the data in each field or column is characterised correctly. If numbers, dates or currency are allocated to the 'text'

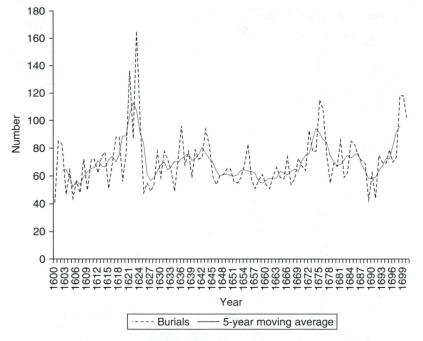

Figure 5.7 Chart showing trends in burials in Ashton, 1600–1700.
Source: Parish register data.

field type it will not be possible to perform calculations on them. More sophisticated spreadsheets allow aids such as data validation to assist in the data entry process. A range of cells may also be designated as a list. By using this function, the data contained in the list may be managed and analysed independently of data outside the designated list.

The main database functions supplied by most spreadsheet programs are: sorting, filtering and querying, and frequency and summary tables.

Sorting

Spreadsheets allow lists of data to be arranged in a number of ways. They may be sorted into ascending or descending order; sorted by the contents of up to three columns (first by sex, then by age, then by occupation) and sorted by rows rather than by columns. This latter function is a special feature of spreadsheets and is not usually available in database programs. A column in a spreadsheet may also be sorted without affecting the order of the other columns on the sheet. This function is useful on occasions but is also troublesome and the unwary user may find that

Table 5.4 A summary table demonstrating voting behaviour and occupational category in the West Riding, 1837 (Tory vote % by constituency)

Occupation	Bradford	Halifax	Huddersfield	Knaresborough
Gentry and professionals	63.1	53.5	49.1	79.3
Merchants and manufacturers	51.2	39.8	47.5	60.9
Skilled craftsmen	44.4	27.5	39.6	55.5
Retailers	43.6	26.8	40.1	58.1
Unskilled and labourers	47.0	55.5	16.7	72.9
Agricultural	52.1	78.3	83.9	63.2

Source: West Riding Elections database.

they have allocated different occupations to the population in their dataset by accident.

Filtering and querying

Spreadsheets often use the term 'filtering' rather than querying to create subsets of the data. This is because rather than using 'querying language' to create a new table it is temporarily 'hiding' the data filtered out in the same table. However, the end results of filtering are the same as performing queries on the dataset. The filtering function allows the user to select data which meet exact criteria, those which do not meet the criteria, to select ranges of information and to use wild cards.

Frequency and summary tables

Most spreadsheet programs allow simple frequency tables to be created to count the number of unique values in a particular column. One, two or three columns may be compared in order to create a cross-tabulation. Spreadsheet tables often have the advantage of allowing different types of summaries to be displayed. For example, in addition to totalling the number of values in each category, the average or count may be displayed. In Table 5.4 a cross-tabulation of constituency, voting behaviour and occupational category has been created from the West Riding database. This demonstrates the fluctuations in the Tory vote when analysed by occupational category.

▶ Presenting information

For many historians, the comprehensive charting functions of spreadsheets are the most effective tools to present a wide range of information. A **graph** usually describes a diagram showing the relationship between two variables each measured along one of a pair of lines called **axes**. **Charts** may be of many different types including pictograms, histograms, cartograms and pie charts. It is important to format tables, graphs and charts correctly:

- all figures, tables, graphs and charts should have an appropriate title;
- the time period and units of measurement should be indicated. Wherever possible, the source of the material contained in the tables and charts should be identified;
- columns, rows, and axes should be clearly labelled and where appropriate the unit of measurement must be given;
- legends or keys should be given where necessary.

Tables, charts and graphs are powerful tools to enable the historian to explain and interpret the results of their analysis. Pictures and charts will often display a mass of numerical information far more effectively than paragraphs of dense prose. It is important to select the most appropriate graph or chart for the information being presented. For example, a pie chart is best suited to data which falls into six or seven categories; a pie chart with 20 slices would be difficult to read. However, in searching for the most suitable chart, the historian needs to be careful that the data presented is not being manipulated or distorted. For instance, by manipulating the scale of the y-axis, the distance between values may be exaggerated unfairly. Most spreadsheet programs allow experimentation so that the user may display the same data in a number of different charts and graphs, this allows the most effective chart to be selected for the data being presented. Once the type of chart has been chosen, the format may be altered for the best possible effect. The following principles should be employed when designing a graph for historical data:

- **Simplicity**: Is the graph communicating information to the reader. If there is too much information displayed or the graph is crowded or cramped it will impede the user.
- **Clarity**: The information on the graph should be interpreted easily. Titles, labels and legends should be precise and succinct. The structure of the graph should be appropriate.
- **Convention**: Consider how other historians have presented similar data. This will enable information on your chart to be compared with that of other scholars.

Bar charts and histograms

Bar charts and **histograms** display data collected from frequency tables. In bar charts the bars are separated from each other and the height of each bar represents

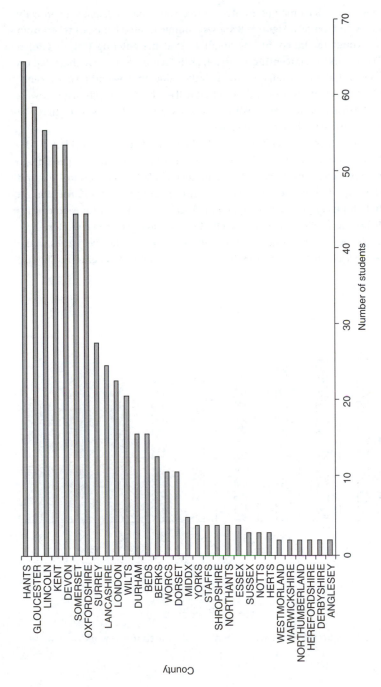

Figure 5.8 Simple rotated bar chart showing the county of origin of students entering Corpus Christi College in the sixteenth century.

Source: Corpus Christi database.

the different values. Bars may be rotated so that the x-axis is displayed vertically and the y-axis horizontally. Figure 5.8 shows a simple rotated bar chart taken from a frequency count of the county of origin of students entering Corpus Christi College, Oxford, in the sixteenth century. If, as in Figure 5.8, the bar chart depicts a frequency count, it is often effective to order the values into ascending or descending order. In this format, the reader of the chart will easily see the highest and lowest values and the distribution of the frequency counts. A three dimensional chart will also accentuate the size of each of the bars.

If there is more than one series of data the bars are usually placed side by side. Figure 5.9 illustrates a bar chart with two series of data presenting the percentage of women employed in the workforce in a number of Western nations in 1960 and in 1996. It is important not to display too many different pieces of information on one graph. If, for example, there was data for female employment for each county per decade between 1900 and 2000, the chart would have been too complex.

For multiple series of data a stacked bar chart may be more effective. This is where each value is placed on top of the one below giving a total of 100 per cent. The size

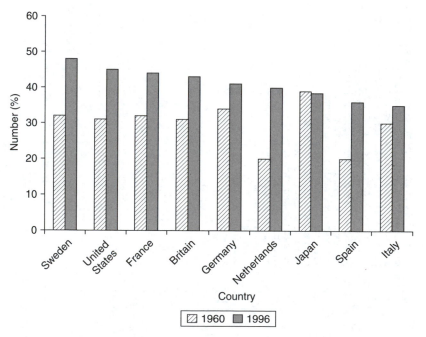

Figure 5.9 A bar chart depicting the percentage of women in the workforce in 1960 and 1996.

Source: OECD.

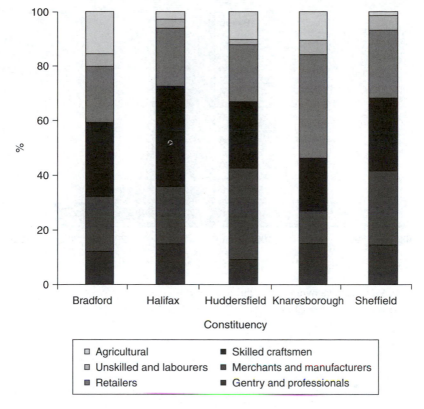

Figure 5.10 A stacked bar chart showing the composition of different West Riding electorates in 1837.

Source: West Riding elections database.

of each segment may be compared across the chart. Figure 5.10 allows a comparison to be drawn of the occupational composition of different West Riding constituencies.

Histograms also show the frequency of data. However, the blocks are drawn so that their areas (rather than their height, as in a bar chart) are proportional to the frequencies within a class or across several class boundaries. In addition there are usually no spaces between the blocks. Figure 5.11 demonstrates an effective use of a histogram. Here, an age pyramid is constructed from the 1881 Harbury census showing the distribution of ages across the population.

Graphs

Simple graphs are usually used by historians for displaying changes in trends over time. A **scatter** or **point** graph (see e.g. Figure 5.12) clearly demonstrates the distribution of values over a period of time.

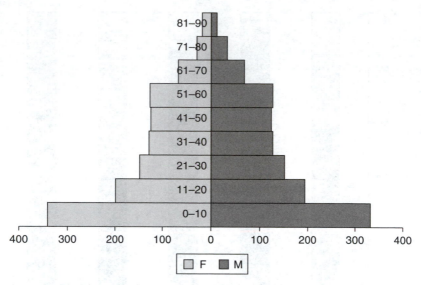

Figure 5.11 An age pyramid for Harbury, 1881.

Source: Harbury census database.

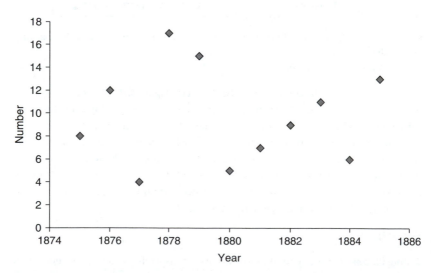

Figure 5.12 A simple scatter graph showing the number of deaths per year of London compositors, 1875–85.

Source: London Society of Compositors, 1890.

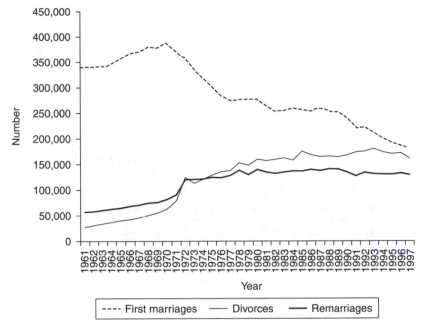

Figure 5.13   A line graph showing the number of first marriages, divorces and remarriages in the UK, 1961–97.

Source: Office of National Statistics.

Line graphs are particularly useful for measuring change over a long period of time. More than one variable may be displayed on the y-axis (see Figure 5.13).

Trend lines may also be added to line graphs in order to indicate the gradient and direction of the trend (see Figure 5.14). If the range of values varies widely or if the types of data on a graph are mixed (such as price and volume), a secondary y-axis may be plotted. Logarithmic scales may also be used if the data plotted contains values that are far apart. A logarithm expresses a number as the exponent of a base value. The most common logarithmic base value is 10: therefore the logarithm of 10 is 1 as 10 to the power of 1 is 10; the logarithm of 100 is 2 since 10 to the power of 2 is 100 and so on. Logarithmic graphs are usually employed to meet the following circumstances:

- the data has very wide ranging values (e.g. television ownership from 1960–2000);
- two or more data sets with differing values are displayed on the same graph (e.g. population figures and numbers of deaths per year);
- for demonstrating relative rates of change. For example, the relative increase from 5 to 10 and from 50 to 100 is the same: both are increases of 100 per cent. Arithmetic graphs display the absolute difference (in this example 5 and 50).

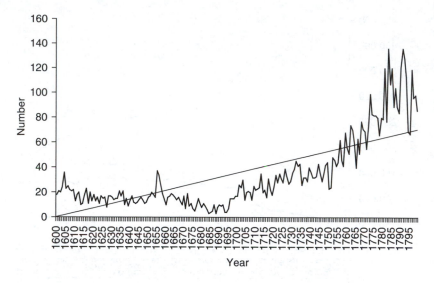

Figure 5.14   A line graph showing the number and trend of marriages in Ashton, 1600–1799.

Source: Parish register data.

Pie charts

Pie charts are most useful for comparing different categories or sets of data with each other. Each sector or slice of the pie depicts a different value. Values may be displayed as absolute values or as percentages. Pie charts may also be three dimensional in order to accentuate the size of each slice (see Figure 5.15).

In order to emphasise the difference between each category further, slices of the pie may be pulled out or exploded. To draw attention to one particular value, just one slice may be singled out in this manner. To see the difference between the categories clearly, all the slices may be pulled apart from each other. In Figure 5.16, the number of printers dying from pneumonia in the late nineteenth century is clearly indicated.

Combination charts

So far, only single chart types have been considered. However, on occasion it may be appropriate to use a combination of chart types on a single graph. This technique emphasises one set of values in comparison with a range of others. For example, Figure 5.17 presents a series of economic data from early twentieth-century Russia. By using columns for the data on electricity output, the reader will find it easier to compare that data with the statistics for other commodities. If all the data had been

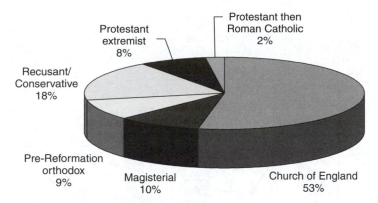

Figure 5.15 A pie chart depicting the religious persuasion of students entering Corpus Christi College in the sixteenth century.

Source: Corpus Christi database.

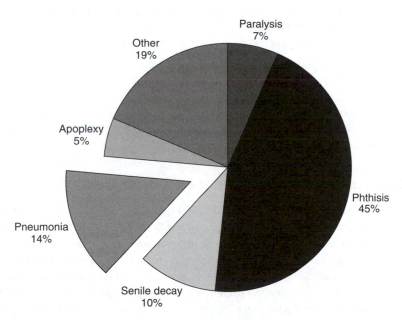

Figure 5.16 A pie chart showing the causes of death of London compositors, 1870–89.

Source: London Society of Compositors, 1890.

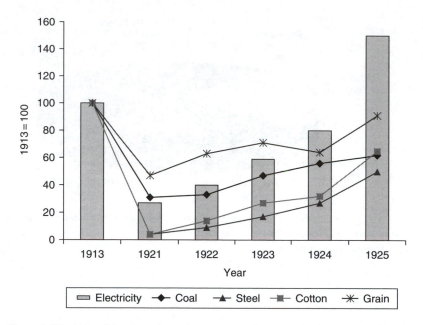

Figure 5.17 A combination chart depicting production of selected commodities before and after the Russian Revolution.

Source: B. R. Mitchell, *European Statistics*, 2nd edn (London, 1981), pp. 232, 388, 409–10, 422, 459 and 501.

displayed as lines or bars, it would have been more difficult to emphasise the performance of the electricity industry compared with other sectors of the Russian economy.

Other diagrams

As well as using formal graphs and charts most spreadsheet programs allow users to depict information pictorially or diagrammatically. Simple pictures and diagrams may be more effective than trying to fit information onto a chart. Alternatively charts may be used in conjunction with pictures to add a further dimension (such as geographical area or space) to the presentation of data. A simple and informative way of presenting a frequency distribution is to use a **pictogram**. By using a book to demonstrate school attendance, Figure 5.18 illustrates how a pictogram may be used to present information clearly.

A more sophisticated combination of pictures and data is the **cartogram** which allows a spatial dimension to be added to the analysis. A simple cartogram is the

Figure 5.18 Pictogram showing school attendance in selected counties in Britain and Ireland in 1851.
Source: 1851 Census.

overlaying of pie charts or bar graphs onto an outline map or even the shading of areas of the map to represent different values (see Figure 5.19). Recently the development of **Geographical Information Systems** (GIS) has allowed more sophisticated spatial analyses to be carried out. GIS were invented in Canada in 1965 to map environmental changes across the country although earlier forms of computerised mapping were developed in the 1950s and 1960s. Historians use GIS to answer a range of questions relating to time and space, for example uncovering disease clusters or measuring voting behaviour. GIS also uncovers relationships between, for example, soil types and disease or altitude and literacy rates. Historical GIS is a growing area and there is specialist software available to create computerised graphs. However, this software is quite complex to use.

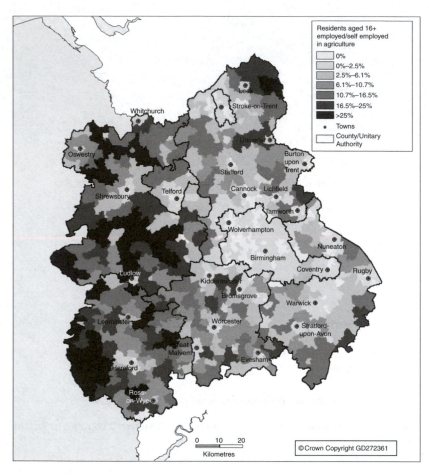

Figure 5.19 Employment in agriculture in the West Midlands, 1996.
Source: Office of National Statistics.

Venn diagrams allow comparisons within a set or subset of data and depict the relationships between them. Therefore, Figure 5.20 considers two subsets from the Harbury census of 1881: females and heads of households, and illustrates the overlap between them.

Other diagrams may be used for simple depictions of data. Figure 5.21 represents the classic interpretation of the business cycle. Chapters 2 and 6 look at other aspects of presentation in more detail.

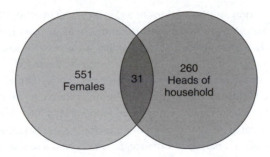

Figure 5.20   Venn diagram depicting female heads of households in Harbury, 1881.
Source: Harbury census database.

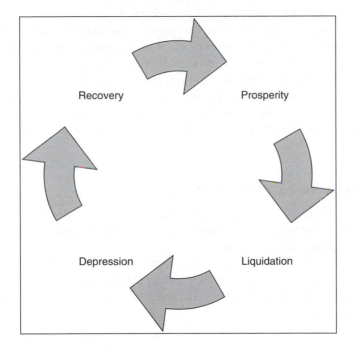

Figure 5.21   The business cycle.

▶ Further study

This chapter has concentrated on the most basic forms of quantitative and statistical analyses utilised by historians. Spreadsheets will allow more sophisticated financial, mathematical and statistical interrogations including measuring asset depreciation, significance testing or returning the kurtosis (the sharpness of a peak compared with a normal distribution) of a dataset. As with all statistical analyses however, it is important to understand the purpose of the operations and apply them appropriately. The spreadsheet will produce an answer without querying the objectives of the process. The answer supplied may be worthless if there has not been adequate consideration of the data in question. It is recommended, therefore that one of the textbooks which consider the quantitative analysis of historical sources is consulted before undertaking more sophisticated interrogations.

To use the full range of statistical analyses including regression, logistic regression, survival analysis, analysis of variance, factor analysis and multivariate analysis, it is necessary to employ one of the specialist statistical analysis packages such as SAS (SAS Institute Incorporated), Stata (Stata Corporation) or SPSS (SPSS Limited). These packages are far more complex than simple spreadsheet programs but have the benefit of allowing analysis of a large number of data files containing an almost unlimited number of variables. They also allow for the statistical analysis of survey data, something not usually offered by spreadsheet programs. The programs use a variety of methods to manipulate data ranging from simple 'point and click' interfaces using pull-down menus to select commands; entering one line commands which are inputted one command at a time; or the full scale production of programs to perform data analysis. All the statistics programs also have powerful graphics facilities which allow the production of highly sophisticated graphs and charts.

▶ Guide to further reading

Darcy, R. and Rohrs, R. C., *A Guide to Quantitative History* (Westport, Ct, 1995).

Feinstein, C. and Thomas, M., *Making History Count: A Primer in Quantitative Methods for Historians* (Cambridge, 2002).

Gregory, I., *A Place in History. A Guide to Using GIS in Historical Research* (AHDS, 2002) and available online from: http://hds.essex.ac.uk/g2gp/gis/index.asp.

Hudson, P., *History by Numbers: An Introduction to Quantitative Approaches* (London, 2000).

6 Digital Texts and Images

The digital revolution has resulted in a mass of digitised historical texts and images becoming available, largely via the World Wide Web. For many historians, the mere fact that texts and images are accessible in a computerised format will be sufficient for them to analyse and manipulate the information for research projects. However, some may wish to use more sophisticated analytical tools and to create their own images for use in projects, essays, dissertations and websites. This chapter provides a basic introduction to the use of digital texts and images for historians.

▶ Computer-based text analysis

Computer-based (or 'computer-aided') text analysis is becoming an important tool for historians although in the past it was used only by specialists. In this brief introduction, we want to give a quick overview of what computer-based text analysis is, and mention its use for the historian. This is by no means a comprehensive guide, and if you decide to use it to mark up your own texts for analysis you will need to take further advice. However, much digitised text is now available in a searchable form. The texts may come from a text archive, a library or some of the burgeoning number of digitised text projects organised by universities, archives or academic publishers. Alternatively you may decide to scan documents yourself and convert them into digital text. If you choose this latter route however, be careful about infringing **copyright** restrictions.

Free text databases

The past decade has seen the emergence of an increasing number of digitised text databases which are available to search and to analyse in similar ways to structured databases (see Chapter 4). Clearly, some of the quantitative analyses possible with structured databases are not appropriate to these free text or free form text archives. However, imaginative use of searching techniques will yield fruitful results. These digitised text sources also allow the analysis of textual sources in ways that were previously impossible. Unfortunately, many of these textual sources are subscription-only, and they are therefore unavailable to the independent researcher who does not have access to the resources of a national or university library. However, there are some excellent freely available searchable text archives. One example is *The Proceedings of the Old Bailey London 1674 to 1834* [http://www.oldbaileyonline.org]. This is a fully searchable online edition of 100,621 criminal trials held at London's central criminal court between 1674 and 1834. Whilst the source is important for historians of crime, it also allows insights into the lives of ordinary (largely) English people from the seventeenth to the nineteenth centuries. Sophisticated searches are available on the occupations, addresses, gender, age, crimes, verdicts and punishments of those mentioned in the proceedings. It is also possible to research members of the judiciary and the lawyers involved. Searches may be carried out on associated texts and there is even an interactive map of London available where the locations of crimes (or other events) may be plotted. The search techniques involved draw on some of the skills discussed in Chapter 3 (pp. 57–59).

The recently launched *Google Scholar* [http://www.scholar.google.com] allows keyword searches on academic material including theses, technical reports, articles, university websites and books. The search results are ranked by order of relevance including the number of citations by other authors, rather than the number of hits the page has received. Many of these resources were not accessible using ordinary search engines. Google has also introduced a programme to digitally scan books from the libraries of Harvard University, Stanford University, the University of Michigan, the University of Oxford and The New York Public Library. This will allow access to material not widely available via the *Google print programme* [http://print.google.com]. The content of the books will be displayed in keeping with copyright law. Rival providers such as Yahoo! have similar services. The *Internet Archive Project* [http://www.archive.org] has also reached agreement with US and Candian libraries to provide information freely in a searchable format over the internet.

There are also important text databases for historians which are only available via subscription. These include Early English Books Online (EEBO) published by ProQuest Information and Learning Company, available at: http://eebo.chadwyck.com/home/. EEBO is a comprehensive digitised collection of every book published in England from 1473 to 1700. It comprises over 125,000 titles containing 22.5 million pages. Relevant literature from fields as diverse as Classics, Astronomy, Poetry, Witchcraft and Belles Lettres is included. Full text searching is available on the titles, authors and publishers and a portion of the texts. EEBO is available free of charge to all UK Universities. A related source is Eighteenth Century Collections Online (ECCO) published by Thomson Gale available at: http://www.gale.com/Eighteenth Century/.

This allows access to over 150,000 texts comprising 33 million pages. The publishers aim to digitise every significant text published in England and the British Empire between 1701 and 1800. All the resources in ECCO are fully searchable.

Early printed newspapers are another useful source which are being targeted by digitisation projects. The ProQuest Historical Newspapers project will contain the full texts of US Historical Newspapers including *The New York Times, The Wall Street Journal, The Washington Post, The Christian Science Monitor, The Los Angeles Times* and the *Chicago Tribune.* These are all searchable and allow access to digitised images of the appropriate newspaper page. ProQuest also have digitised collections of UK, Australian and New Zealand newspapers. Thomson Gale publish a digitised text of *The Times* at http://www.galegroup.com/Times/ from 1785 to 1985. These projects allow newspapers to be used in innovative ways for research purposes. Previously, researchers had to rely on outdated indexes and/or ploughing through reams of print on the screen of a microfilm reader. The newspapers may be searched for names or events or for categories such as news, editorial or adverts. This ability to search immense quantities of text quickly and efficiently opens up the newspapers as a resource for a wide range of historical studies. However, errors do appear in the recognition of text which is often blurred and indistinct in the original copy. It may sometimes be advisable to employ fuzzy matching techniques to achieve the best results.

A final resource to mention in this brief overview of free text databases is the *Oxford Dictionary of National Biography* [http://www.oxforddnb.com]. This project contains articles on people who were born and lived in the British Isles, people from Britain who achieved recognition in other countries, people who lived in territories connected to Britain at one stage of their history, and people born elsewhere who settled in Britain for significant periods. It contains over 50,000 articles of people who died before 2001. The advanced search tool available with the website allows innovative research techniques. These include the ability to search for images, for people connected with particular religious groups, or for people alive or active at certain periods of time in particular locations. The site also allows free text searching. For example, to locate biographies containing the word "murderer" or "rebel".

What is computer-based text analysis?

If the text you wish to search is not available in one of these text archives then you may wish to prepare it for analysis yourself using a proprietary programme. In brief, computer-based text analysis allows you do identify some of the main themes of a text. In that sense, you might think that it is vaguely similar to the 'Auto-Summarize' function of recent versions of Microsoft Word. However, it is more powerful than that, and gives you greater control over what actually happens.

Comparing it to a word-processing package is quite useful for understanding what computer-based text analysis can do. A word-processing package allows you to identify some themes in a text; but it will not let you investigate in detail why these are the themes or where they occur. Similarly, a word-processor will allow you (through the 'Find' function) to find certain words in a text, but it will not give you a survey of how often that word occurs, or its relationship to other words. Computer-based text analysis can do both these things.

How does it work?

The success of computer-aided text analysis depends on how much work you are prepared to put into it. What we describe here is the most basic way of using a simple version of such a tool. It only gives you a small range of results and insights, but then you don't have to work hard to get these results, either.

Assume you have a historical text in electronic format. You can essentially 'feed' this text into the text analysis program with minimal preparation (more about that in a moment) and the program will return to you a selection of information about this text.

At its most basic level, a computer-based text analysis program will index your document; that is, it will take account of every word in it and where that word is.

If you are prepared to invest more time, you can expand the functions of computer-based text analysis considerably, but this brief overview is not the place to discuss this.

How can it be useful for a historian?

Computer-based text analysis comes into its own when you deal with very long documents. A medieval chronicle, for instance, or a diary, or a nineteenth-century novel. Imagine that you want to identify the main preoccupations of the bishop who wrote the verse history of the Scottish Wars of Independence. You may have read the work and formed some definite opinions of his political or spiritual agenda, but computer-based text analysis can show you exactly where the words and phrases which support these views appear, and it may have some surprises in store by identifying other key words which he uses just as frequently, but whose significance has been overlooked. Analysing a nineteenth-century novel in a similar way may throw up some common social themes of the time, or, once again, show what themes were particularly dear to the author's heart. The frequent use of particular adjectives, especially if they repeatedly show in conjunction with a particular noun, can tell you a lot about the conscious or subconscious agenda of the author – something you might have missed in the sea of words on a normal reading. Another rich field for computer-based text analysis is recent government documentation, in particular speeches and debates and policy documents.

How is it set up?

There are a number of text-analysis packages available. A very basic freely available program is TACT which will enable you to make an introduction to the process. TACT has the advantage of having a web-based version, so that you can experiment with it at your leisure without installing anything on your computer, before you decide whether or not it is the right program for you. However, TACT is also a very old program, and while it does its job very well, it runs on an interface which you may consider strange and a little intimidating. It is not really difficult to use, but it comes from the pre-Windows era and therefore it *looks* as though it is complicated, simply because the friendly interface everybody has become used to is missing. And you cannot use a mouse with it – it is all keyboard-based. The Web interface, however, is very user-friendly and makes a good first stop for those who want to explore the program.

You can find the TACT installation files at: ftp://chass.utoronto.ca/pub/cch/tact/tact2.1/. The web-based version can be accessed at: http://tactweb.mcmaster.ca/ and we would recommend experimenting with that first of all.

If you decide that you want to analyse your electronic text in TACT, you will have to '**model**' it. This means adding '**mark-up**'. Essentially, what this means is that you have to decide which parts of your text are particularly important to you; how you want to structure the results. For instance if you are analysing a diary, you might want to 'mark-up' each separate date so that when your results are displayed, you can see whether they cluster around particular times. If you are analysing the content of government debates, you might want to mark-up each individual speaker so that your results will show who uses certain terminology more than others.

If you have ever seen any **HTML**, you'll know what mark-up looks like – the principles of all mark-up language are essentially the same. Again, it looks strange and complex, but it is really a simple procedure. Possible elements to identify are: books, chapters, acts, scenes, speakers, personal names, concepts. Obviously, the more of these individual items you want to mark-up, the more complex your task becomes and the longer it will take. Of course it may also make your analysis much more powerful.

After marking-up your text, you have to go through various steps to convert it into a format which the TACT software can read. Further instructions for doing this come with the TACT download you can get from ftp://chass.utoronto.ca/pub/cch/tact/tact2.1/.

What can you do with it?

Within TACT, there are four main ways in which you can analyse your text without investing much time in preparing it.

The Word List

The simplest type of display TACT will give you is the **Word List**. You don't even have to use mark-up for this. Rather predictably, the Word List is a list of all the words in the text. It is a simple means of discovering which words are used a lot in a text, and which hardly at all.

The Keyword in Context (KWIC) Display

The **KWIC** Display will show you all occurrences of a particular word that you have searched for, with a line of context attached. This way, you get a very quick overview of the way a word is used by the author. It is also a very useful way of finding a particular occurrence which you vaguely remember but cannot quite pinpoint anymore.

The word you search for will itself usually be displayed in the middle of the line, with a few words to either side of it. Depending on the mark-up you used, there will also be some information at the start of the line about which line, chapter, book or date point the word occurred at.

The Variable Context Display

Seeing a single line is enough to give you an idea of the most common uses of a word, but sometimes it is not enough. The **Variable Context** Display gives you greater control over just how much you want to see – whether two, four, or ten lines around each word. It still means that you do not have to flip to the full text to see what is going on, but gives you more information than a simple KWIC display would. Especially with authors who use long, convoluted sentences, getting a standard three lines through the Variable Context Display can be more useful than a KWIC display.

Depending on how you have marked-up your text, you can select more than just a number of lines. For example, assuming you marked-up each day separately in a diary you are analysing, you could select to see a day either side of the occurrence of a particular word. Obviously this could lead to some very big displays, so it is best to be cautious with this.

The Distribution Graph

A distribution graph will give you a quick overview of where exactly in a text any chosen word or string appears. You will not see the text associated with it, but you will see whether an author became preoccupied with a particular issue at a certain point in his or her text. The **Distribution Graph** will subdivide the text into blocks of 10 per cent, and give you the figures, as well as a very simple graphical display, for the occurrences of your chosen word within each of these blocks. You might use this, for instance, to find that a chronicler was concerned with livestock in the first third of his text, but not in the second.

The Collocation search

Collocates are words which occur in the text close to the keyword you defined/searched for. You can set the parameters of what counts as 'close' – whether it is within three words or within five words, for example. You can then measure the **Collocate Frequency**, which will tell you how often each collocate is used close to your term. You can also measure the **Type Frequency**, which tells you how many times each collocate is used in the entire text of the work you are analysing. Following on from that, you have something called the **Z-score** which uses collocate frequency and type frequency together to indicate how likely it is that the collocation of any particular two words is actually significant. For instance, if the word 'liberty' occurs within three words of 'fraternity' twenty times in your text (the collocate frequency), that would appear to be significant. However, if 'liberty' was used a total of four hundred times in the overall text (the type frequency), then the fact that twenty of these times it was adjacent to 'fraternity' is no longer quite so outstanding. Therefore, perhaps the collocation is not quite as significant as we first thought.

The Web version of TACT at: http://tactweb.humanities.mcmaster.ca/tactweb/doc/tact.htm has a workbook and guide which will let you try out the various methods described here on prepared samples of text.

TACT is of course not the only available text analysis program. A list of other programs, partly more sophisticated, often more modern and usually more expensive is available here: http://www.textanalysis.info/inforet.htm. If experimenting with TACT makes you realise that this kind of analysis could be useful for your studies, you may want to look into more elaborate programs such as WordSmith (available at http://nora.hd.uib.no/wordsmith/) or freeform database type programs such as AskSam (available from http://www.asksam.com/). These packages allow the integration of images and other media, as well as text, into your database.

▶ Further study

A more recent development in text analysis is the use of **XML**. XML stands for 'Extensible Mark-up Language' – it belongs to the same family as (Hypertext Mark-up Language) which is used for Web pages, and **SGML** (Standard Generalized Mark-up Language) which is often used by cataloguers. XML is one of the most flexible forms of mark-up language around and is increasingly being used for everything from online car dealer catalogues to historical data manipulation and text analysis.

The advantage of XML over previous forms of mark-up languages is that you can invent your own terms. Where HTML, for example, had a limited range of codes with fixed meanings, XML has recommended fields and unlimited potential for 'extension' – hence the name. Its advantage over ordinary databases is that you do not have to standardise your actual data for input into a category field, since you merely type your mark-up into the existing document; that way your text stays intact, and the category/categories are only represented in the mark-up.

Using XML for text analysis allows you, much as TACT, to mark up any word, phrase, or section of text and classify it. However, it is more powerful than TACT in that you can have nested classifications (mark-ups within mark-up). It is also, arguably, the way of the future.

Having said this, using XML for text analysis is not easy. The process is still new, simple readers of marked-up text do not yet exist, and you need a fair level of technical knowledge. We are simply mentioning it here as something to keep an eye on if you ever intend to get serious about historical text analysis.

For some more information see:

http://xml.coverpages.org/heml.html
http://xml.coverpages.org/ni2002-04-06-a.html
http://www.w3.org/XML/

▶ Acquiring and manipulating digital images

First, get your image

While you are putting together your dissertation or presentation, there may come a point when an image can say more than a thousand words. This is the point where you venture into new territory – for while word-processing, spreadsheets and databases each have separate functions and characteristics, at least you are dealing with characters and figures and a generally standardised, recognisable environment.

Images are something else altogether. First of all, there is the issue of getting one. Essentially, you have two options: you take a pre-existing image; or you produce your own. The latter is very much recommended, because that will help you avoid the complex questions of **copyright** which using somebody else's image inevitably raises. But let us for a moment assume that you have to find and use an image owned by somebody else. There are a few ways of doing this.

General Web search

Google has an image search facility [http://images.google.com/], and this could well be your first stop. Be careful, though, to find out where the image you are presented with really comes from. You cannot just take an image off the Web and use it in your own publication or presentation, because you will leave yourself open to prosecution by the owner. You should try to find out who the owner is, contact them, and ask for permission to use the image. Unless this is the only copy of the image available, it is probably more hassle than it is worth.

Targeted Web search

There are some sites which will make images available for non-commercial or educational use. You may want to check the *'Modern History Image Bank' at Brooklyn College* [http://academic.brooklyn.cuny.edu/history/core/pics/] or more general links from the *Internet Modern History Sourcebook* [http://www.fordham.edu/halsall/mod/modsbook.html]. For Medieval and Classical studies, the *'Exploring Ancient World Cultures Index of Internet Resources'* [http://eawc.evansville.edu/index.htm] points to useful repositories. The *'Internet Ancient History Sourcebook'* [http://www.fordham.edu/halsall/ancient/asbook.html] links to a number of websites which offer images with varying levels of copyright permission. If you are lucky, you will find what you need on one of these sites. If you do, remember that you should credit the copyright-holders who generously provide copyright-permitted images. You can find out how to do this at *'Give Credit'* [http://www.givecredit.com/]. As a rule of thumb, copyright credit should appear on the same page as the copyrighted image.

A complication to consider, though, is that this kind of permission for using images normally applies if you want to use an image to teach – for instance, you can put it in your presentation, on a course website or in a handout. You are *not* normally supposed to use it in a print publication, and if you are planning to do anything of the kind, it is recommended that you write to or e-mail the copyright holder to be sure where you stand.

Scanning images from books

Scanning is an even more complex and potentially distressing issue. If you scan an image from a publication and then use it in any publication of your own, it is likely that you will be infringing the copyright of three people or institutions – the author, the publisher, and the photographer who took the picture in the first place. None of them will be pleased.

Of course you can always identify the copyright holder and offer to pay to use the image. This may be a last resort in cases where you need a particular image, or where the object depicted no longer exists so you cannot go and take your own. *Ligon's Webpage Toolbox'* [http://www.ncsu.edu/mega/cipe/Media/Bytes/toolbox.html] provides form letters you can use for this.

NOTE: It is important to bear in mind that even if you have paid to use an image which is copyrighted by somebody else, this does not give you the right to change the image in any way – for example, you cannot just choose to use a detail from it. This would involve a different form of copyright clearance.

Your own images

On the whole, it is much simpler to use an image you have taken yourself. It may be a photograph, a slide, or you may be lucky and already have a digital image.

Scanning from photographs

This is a very straightforward process. Scanners are cheap these days, and most of them have default settings which are easy to use. Simply follow the instructions which come with them. In most cases, you simply place the photograph face-down on the glass panel of the scanner, close the lid and press the 'scan' button on the scanner or, alternatively, click 'scan' in your on-screen software. Many scanners will initially scan the entire area (usually A4 or US letter size), no matter how big your image actually is. This is called the 'pre-scan'. Once this is done, you can normally just click and drag to identify the area which you actually want. Then click 'scan' again, and this time the area you selected will be scanned.

Many scanners will allow you to manipulate the scanned image in other ways at this point. You can, for example, change the brightness or contrast settings, or rotate the image. You may want to experiment with this a little.

After you are satisfied, save the image to a place you can remember. Many scanners set up their own predetermined place where they want to store the image, but this may not be the place where you really want it. The easiest thing to do is probably to save to the 'My Images' folder in Windows, if you are on a Windows platform. If you are a more experienced user, we recommend that you set yourself up with a new folder in a place you can easily find (and will remember to back up regularly) and choose to save all your images there.

Scanning from slides

Scanning from a slide is essentially the same as scanning from a photograph, except for the fact that you have to buy a separate attachment for your scanner which will allow you to feed the slide into it. Make sure that you buy a scanner for which such an attachment can be provided. After that, the process is essentially the same as for a photograph.

Using a digital camera

If the object you want to depict is still in existence and accessible, this is the simplest way of getting exactly what you want. Most digital cameras are very simple to operate – really very similar to conventional point-and-click cameras – and will give you high-quality files to work with. If you have print publication in mind, the only thing to make sure of right away is that your photos are taken at a fairly high **resolution** level (see more on resolution below). Your camera user manual will tell you how to pick the correct setting. The images can then be transferred from your camera to your computer by various means which will depend on the camera you have. Again, the relevant instructions will be provided with your equipment.

So now you have an image on your computer ...

Your image, whether scanned or downloaded, may not be in the format you want, need or that is most practical for the intended use. For instance, while you will want to retain as much resolution as possible for an image that will be printed, it is a good idea to keep the file sizes of Web images as small as possible, and therefore resolution may have to be compromised. Another way of reducing file size is to cut out irrelevant parts of the image.

What you do with your image next depends on what you want to use it for. The simplest rule of thumb is that for print publication, you want it to be very finely grained and detailed; for a Powerpoint presentation, you will aim for a happy medium between detail and file size; and finally, for Web publication, size (or rather the lack of it) matters, and you may have to sacrifice some detail. This is where 'Resolution' comes in.

Resolution

Resolution determines how detailed your image really is; how much 'information' is contained in it. Digital cameras and scanners are usually priced and sold by how much 'resolution' they can give you. It is often measured in '**megapixels**'. A pixel is simply a tiny dot which is part of all the tiny dots which eventually make up the full image. If an image is 10 cm by 10 cm and contains 100,000 dots, you have a lower resolution than if the same image contains 1,000,000 dots. 1,000,000 dots can clearly store the information in a much finer format. To the naked eye, there may not be much of a difference between the two – once the pixels get into absurdly large numbers, there generally is not – but it does have implications for how far you can zoom in on details in the picture, and for how well it will enlarge or print.

This is why you will come across measurements such as '**ppi**' (pixels per inch) or '**dpi**' (dots per inch). The higher the number, the higher the image resolution. For images that are to be printed, aim for the highest possible image resolution.

Note that if you are scanning your own images, you will get the best results if you set the resolution at scanning time rather than changing it later.

File format

Before you start manipulating an image, you should save it to **TIFF** format, even if it is not the format you want to use in the end. TIFF is a format in which all the information which your image originally contained is kept uncompressed and unchanged. Many scanners will save to a different format, **JPEG**, by default. JPEG is a very useful format for Web publication, but if you need high-quality images, it is problematic. Because JPEG compresses the image, using something called 'lossy' compression, you lose a little more of the information contained in your image every time you re-save to JPEG. Obviously, if you are in the process of changing various things about your image, you will be saving it frequently. Losing data every time you do that is not helpful.

Therefore, save the image to TIFF by using the drop-down list in any graphics application (see 'changing file formats' below), and for good measure take a copy of the image just in case something goes wrong. Save the original to **CD-ROM** or **floppy disk** and keep it safe. Now you are ready to play with the copy.

Applications

Most graphics applications, such as Paintshop Pro (by Jasc Software, http://www. jasc.com/) or Adobe Photoshop [http://www.adobe.com/] and a number of smaller and much cheaper options, will allow you to perform a variety of useful manipulations:

- resizing,
- cropping,
- 'zooming',
- colour adjustments,
- conversion.

Resizing

Your image may be far too large for the page. The file size may be too big for the website. Or you may simply have a particular size for the image in mind, and you want it to conform to that.

All image software has a Resize function. In Paintshop Pro, one of the most popular graphics software applications, you access it through Image>Resize. Once you have clicked this, you will find yourself confronted with a multitude of options (see Figure 6.1).

The top option, 'Pixel size', is best ignored unless you have a good idea what you are doing. Going down the range, 'Percentage of original' is straightforward and good for experimenting with. Note that as long as you keep the box right at the bottom of this dialogue box ticked ('Maintain aspect ratio ...'), the proportions of your image will always remain the same, and if you give a percentage for the Width of the image, it will be mirrored by the percentage for Height automatically.

Generally, it is very advisable to keep the ticks in both the 'Resize all layers' and the 'Maintain aspect ratio' boxes.

If you know exactly what size your image needs to be, though, you can tick the 'Actual/print size' button and select a precise Width and Height. Bear in mind that

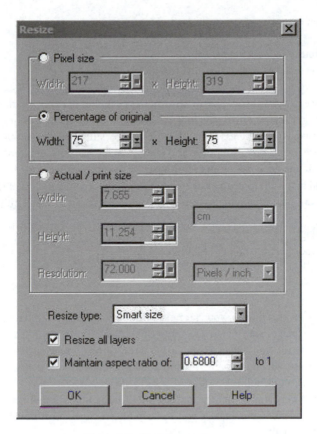

Figure 6.1   Resizing an image.

this can cause some distortion if your original has different proportions. As long as you keep the 'Aspect Ratio' box ticked, adjusting the Width settings in this section will bring up the correct Height settings suggestion which will allow you to keep the image proportions as they were in the original, but if you decide to change the Height settings to something you prefer, the proportion link will be broken.

Finally, you could resize by changing the resolution. This is a very common way of preparing an image for presentation on the Web, or sending it as an attachment to email. Changing resolution is generally a one-way process: you can always *reduce* resolution, but once you have done that and saved the result, it may be difficult to reverse. Be careful before using this.

Reducing resolution means that the number of pixels in your image is reduced – as discussed above, this means that information is lost from your image. The reason this option comes up under 'resize' is twofold:

a. it obviously reduces the *file size*
b. it reduces the *actual* size at which the image will display well.

On the face of it, the image size in centimetres or inches does not change, but you will find that the image no longer looks so good at a larger size because it will appear blurry or pixellated, whereas at smaller sizes it may still look crisp enough.

Of course, Resize has its flipside, and if your image has good enough resolution you can put it to good use: by enlarging a part of the image you can use it as a **zoom**. You would first want to **crop** away (see below) all the irrelevant parts of the image; next you can take what remains and enlarge it to bring out its detail properly.

Cropping

The crop tool in Paintshop Pro looks like this:

If you click on this button, you can next click on your image and drag the mouse to select the image area you want to *keep* – this will be the area bounded by the lines you draw. Once you have selected this area, simply double-click on it and everything else will disappear. If you find you have inadvertently deleted too much, simply click Edit>Undo.

'Crop' is a very useful tool for making sure that you only present the relevant parts of an image; it also enables you to keep file size as small as possible without losing image quality.

Reducing file size for on-screen display

If your image is only intended for display on a screen, whether through a website or because you are planning to send it to somebody as an attachment, you do not need high resolution. A computer screen can only display around 72 dots per inch (dpi) and anything higher than that is wasted. You could therefore go back into Resize and enter 72 pixels/inch in the Resolution box. The other values will adjust automatically. Then click OK. Depending on your starting resolution, it may reduce the file size dramatically (see Figure 6.2).

Colour adjustments

PaintShop Pro, a powerful program in a reasonable price range, offers a great variety of possibilities for making your image look better, or just different. If you click on 'Colours' on the Paintshop Pro toolbar, a drop-down menu will offer you more

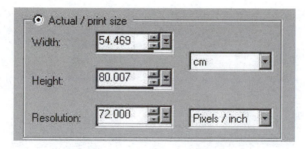

Figure 6.2   Reducing size of images.

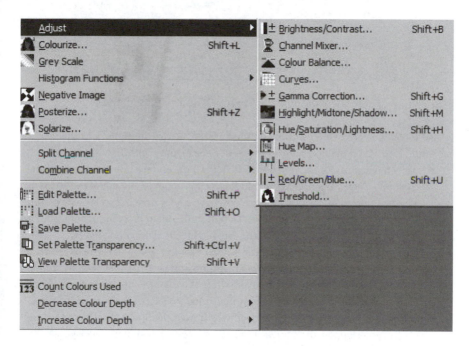

Figure 6.3   Adjusting images.

options than you will know what to do with. It is well worth exploring all of them, but the most straightforward, as well as most obviously useful, ones are the ones which let you lighten or darken an image (see Figure 6.3).

Click Colours, then select 'Adjust', and you will find the Brightness/Contrast function. This is probably the most useful one when you are starting out. You will

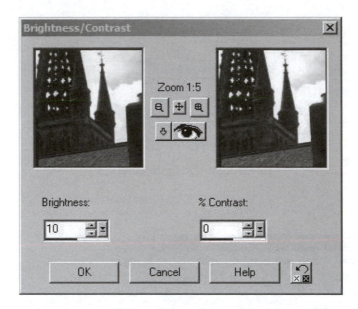

Figure 6.4 Adjusting the brightness and contrast of images.

get a dialogue box which shows you your image as it currently is, and the way it would look if you made certain adjustments (see Figure 6.4):

You can change the settings right in this dialogue box, and see how the image will be affected. The 'Zoom' function in the middle lets you zoom in and out of the image to get a better impression. Eventually, once you have settled on a particular setting, you simply click 'OK'. You can still undo the action in the main program (Edit>Undo) if you decide, upon seeing the result in the 'big picture', that you don't like it.

The other functions work in a very similar fashion – you are usually given a dialogue box like this so you can get an impression of what it is you are doing. A powerful graphics program like Paintshop Pro has too many options to be considered in detail here, but we recommend that you experiment with the possibilities on offer. Another menu item well worth investigating is the 'Effects' menu, which lets you sharpen and blur and image (among other things). See Figure 6.5.

Conversion – changing file formats

Again, different file formats have different size implications. Some are also better for certain things than for others. Here is a rule of thumb involving the major formats currently in use:

TIFF – has no compression, no data loss, is good for archive copies and for working on images which you have to save frequently.

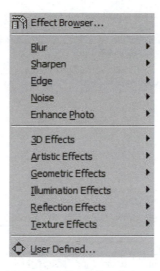

Figure 6.5   The 'Effects' menu.

GIF – is a compressed format but does not lose your data the way JPEG does. It is best for images with plain colours (e.g. cartoons or signs) but not so good for displaying photographs.

JPEG – is a very effective compressed format but loses data every time you save. It is best for photographs and similar images.

GIF and JPEG are used for displaying images on the Web. If you start out with a TIFF, you will find that simply saving it as GIF or JPEG will reduce its file size considerably.

The way to change your image from one file format to another is to start the Save process. Once you have done that, the options usually appear in a drop-down menu. So click File > Save As, and something like the following box will appear:

Depending on what you select, the 'Options ...' button to the right of the drop-down box will offer you ways of customizing the compression settings, and for JPEG you can even access a preview of what your settings will achieve, or a Wizard which helps you decide exactly which option to go for. It is well worth exploring.

▶ Web pages

For many people the reason to create digital texts and images will be to provide content for Web pages.

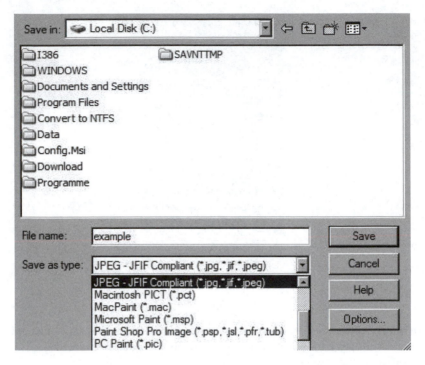

Figure 6.6 Changing the format of an image.

It is quite easy nowadays to make your own webpage. The three main ways of doing it are:

1. Use HTML or a related markup system, perhaps with the help of an HTML editor such as CoffeeCup; most people think this is difficult, but in reality knowledge of only a dozen or so markup codes will enable you to put together a decent webpage, and the code will be much cleaner than that provided by any of the other methods.
2. Use a dedicated Web design editor with a **WYSIWYG** (what you see is what you get) graphical interface, such as Macromedia®'s Dreamweaver® or Microsoft's Frontpage®; this makes webpage creation almost as simple as writing an ordinary document, but offers a range of additional features.
3. Create a document file in an office software application such as Microsoft Word, and choose the 'Save to HTML' option – this results in messy code, but does the job quickly.

Once you have your page, you will of course have to find a place to put it so that others can access it. Within an academic institution, you may be able to take advantage of the university servers to host your page (if you are authorized to do so). Alternatively, pay-for and free hosting services are available on the internet. If you have a private email address, it may well come with free webspace attached.

Whilst it is not our intention to provide a full guide to the design and creation of websites here, a number of 'best practice' hints should be borne in mind:

- Web pages should generally be fast to download. Therefore do not include too many images and follow the tips above for reducing the size of images.
- If you absolutely have to display a large image at high resolution, it is good practice to offer users a much smaller, low-resolution version (a so-called '**thumbnail**') of it first, and invite them to click on that to access the larger version.
- The site should have good navigation aids and a simple structure. The hierarchy of pages should be logical and straightforward. It is often best to sketch out the design of the site on paper first. The home page should have links to a variety of levels and it should be clear how each page fits into the hierarchy.
- Use page titles which will appear on the title bar of the website to aid navigation. Since the page title determines the wording of the Bookmark or Favorite, this will also ensure that readers can easily create meaningful bookmarks for your page.
- Avoid having too much content per page so that readers have to scroll down through reams of text to find what they require. However, 'academic' users are more willing than others to read pages of dense text.
- Under no circumstances force your readers to scroll right to read text that goes beyond the right-hand margin of their screen. Since HTML auto-adjusts to screen width by default, this should not usually be a problem, but if you decide to get fancy with fixed fonts sizes and table cells, problems may occur.
- Do not overcrowd pages with too many links or pieces of information.
- Avoid using too many 'special effects' which may put off users or make the page unwieldy and slow to load.
- Keep the site up to date.
- Make sure your links work. If you change the structure of your site be aware that many internal links may need changing. Check external links regularly to ensure they still work.
- Check **data protection** and **copyright** rules (see Chapter 1) and that your site does not infringe any other legal restrictions.

▶ Guide to further reading

Robinson, P., *The digitisation of primary textual sources* (Oxford, 1993).
Robinson, P., *The transcription of primary textual sources using SGML* (Oxford, 1994).

Glossary

Active cell   The cell currently being worked on.

Animation   The option of setting objects in Powerpoint to appear in a certain sequence and a certain fashion.

Anti-virus software   Software that scans a computer's memory and disk drives for viruses. If viruses are found the application may clean, delete or quarantine any files, directories or disks affected by the code.

Applet   A small program that may be embedded in a Web page.

ASCII   American Standard Code for Information Interchange. A standard for text files which allows computers to exchange and display data. ASCII files do not include any formatting such as bold, italics or underline.

Attributes   The characteristics of each entity.

Auto Shape   A selection of pre-set shapes which Powerpoint offers for you to draw onto your slides.

Average   A measure of central tendency of a list of values.

Axes   The x-axis is usually the horizontal line on a graph, the y-axis is usually the vertical line on a graph.

Back up   The process of creating duplicate copies of data to guard against damage or loss.

Bar chart   A series of horizontal bars or columns on a graph used to measure frequency distributions.

Block quotation   A quotation offset from the main text with paragraph spacing and indents.

Bookmark   In browsers, a way of setting your program to remember a Web address. Also called 'Favorite'. In Word, a placeholder which links to a location on another page and will turn into whichever page number this location will be on.

Boolean operators   Logical operators: AND, OR, NOT. Terms used to include or exclude key words in advanced Web searches.

Browser   Application to view information on the World Wide Web.

Cartogram   A map which contains graphs or pie charts to analyse information spatially.

Categorisation   To arrange information according to a set of criteria.

CD-ROM   A medium for the electronic storage of data.

CD writers   These provide the capacity to write to a CD-ROM.

Cell   A box at the intersection of a row and a column to enter text or numbers in a spreadsheet program.

Cell address   A unique label which identifies a cell usually in the form A6 or Z229.

Chart   A general term describing a range of graphs and diagrams.

Chart area   The container for a Powerpoint chart. Important because sometimes its boundaries aren't very clear, and whether or not you are in it will affect the right-click menu you will be offered.

Codes   Associates text values with numerical or textual codes for ease of analysis.

Coefficient of correlation   A statistical measure of the relationship between two variables. A positive correlation is where the two sets of variables increase or decrease proportionately and simultaneously. A negative correlation is where one variable increases in the same proportion that the other decreases. A perfect positive correlation is $+1$, a perfect negative correlation is -1.

Collocate Frequency   A measure of how often one word is used close to another.

Collocates   Words which occur in a text close to a defined keyword.

Cookie   A piece of information sent by an external Web server to a user's browser.

Copyright   Protects the rights of authors and creators. Something to be taken into account whenever you plan to use somebody else's materials (especially images) in your own work.

Correlation   The association between two variables.

Cross Tabulation   Cross tabulations calculate a sum, average, count, or other type of total for data that is grouped by two types of information. The information is presented in a table with one set of data providing the rows and the other the columns.

Count   The number of unique items in a list.

Cropping   Cutting away unnecessary parts of a digital image.

Data   Information.

Data cleaning   A series of checking procedures after data entry to ensure the integrity of the data.

Data entry   Inputting of information into a database using forms or tables.

Data model   The representation of the structure and relationships in a database.

Data modelling   A methodology used in order to structure information for use in a database.

Data protection   Legislation protecting the rights of individuals whose names and details are held by other organisations, either on paper or electronically.

Data set   A related collection of information.

Data type   The characteristics of a field, cell or column in a database or spreadsheet program.

Database   A collection of related information which may be structured or unstructured. The term may also apply to the program used to analyse the information.

Database management system   The program which constructs and analyses a database.

Default   The settings a program will give you automatically when you first start it up. Usually, the default for most things can be changed.

Distribution Graph   A simple text analysis tool which divides the text into equal blocks to highlight where a word occurs more or less frequently.

Domain   The place where a website is located and always the last part of the Web address. Educational domains are, for example, .ac.uk, or .edu.

Dots per inch (dpi)   A measure of resolution for digital images.

Drag and drop   A mechanism for moving text and images. The object is selected using the mouse, then dragged to a new location which is secured by releasing the mouse button.

Draw Object   A selection of objects which Powerpoint offers for you to draw onto your slides. See also Auto Shape.

Dynamic   Data which is changing.

Dynamic Hyper Text Mark-up Language (DHTML)   Combines HTML, style sheets, and scripts to make Web pages dynamic or interactive.

E-mail   Electronic mail: messages which may be sent from one computer to another.

Entities   Groups of information in a database referring to objects or events.

Entity Relationship Modelling (ERM)   A methodology employed when designing a database. It identifies the entities in a set of data and lists the relationships between the entities.

Favorite   In browsers, a way of setting your program to remember a Web address. Also called 'Bookmark'.

Field   A databases column in a data table. In Word, a piece of code you can insert to update automatically, for instance to reflect page numbers or bookmarks.

Firewall A firewall prevents computers on a network from communicating directly with external computer systems if they do not conform to pre-configured rules.

Flash memory stick A data storage device that connects to the USB port on a computer. It typically provides 64 MB, 128 MB or 256 MB of storage and may be used to back-up computers.

Flat-file Data that is contained in a single table.

Floppy disk A medium for the electronic storage of data.

Footer The section at the bottom of your document in which you can write information to be repeated on every page. Most frequently used for page numbers.

Free form database An unstructured database consisting of digitised text and/or other media which may be searched. Also known as a free text database.

Free text database An unstructured database consisting of digitised text and/or other media which may be searched. Also known as a free form database.

Frequency The number of times a particular value appears in a list.

File Transfer Protocol (ftp) Set of conventions which allow the transfer of files from one computer to another.

Fuzzy matching Matches data which nearly meet specified criteria as well as those which meet them perfectly.

General directory A website which holds links to other websites, grouped thematically.

Geographical Information Systems (GIS) A system that links digitised maps with databases to allow the spatial analysis and presentation of data.

GIF A compressed image file format. Recommended for images with large areas of one colour, or for drawings.

Graph A diagram showing the relationship between two variables each measured along one of a pair of lines called axes.

Grouping   In Powerpoint, the facility which lets you link various objects together as a group, so you can manipulate or animate them as one single object.

Hanging indent   A paragraph format which indents every line of a paragraph *except* the first line. Useful for bibliographies.

Header   The section at the top of your document in which you can write information to be repeated on every page.

Histogram   A chart which measures the frequency of data. The columns or blocks are drawn so that their areas are proportional to the frequencies within a class or across several class boundaries.

HTML   Hypertext Markup Language. The standard underlying framework of webpages.

Hyperlink   A link from a webpage, document page or Powerpoint slide to a website. Can be inserted easily, but to use it, you will have to be connected to the Internet.

Internet   A global collection of computer networks that communicate together.

JPEG   A lossy, compressed image file format. Very effective for reducing file size in preparation for online publication, but unsuitable for repeated manipulation and saving.

KWIC   Key Word In Context. A form of text analysis display which shows all occurrences of a word surrounded by some context.

Legend   On a graph, a key showing the information contained in each line, column or slice.

Line graph   Usually used to measure change over time, it joins together the points plotted for two (or more) sets of variables.

Lookup table   A table that contains a list of allowed entries for a particular table and field.

Many-to-many relationships   Where records from two tables have relationships between them.

Mark-up   Code that is used to tell a computer that certain terms are to be treated specially. Used in text analysis, webpage creation and other contexts.

Maximum   The highest value.

Mean   Also known as arithmetic mean. A calculation of an average by adding together a list of values and then dividing by the number of values.

Median   A calculation of an average by ranking a list of values in order and then taking the middle value.

Megapixel   A measure of resolution for digital cameras.

Meta data   Information about data.

Minimum   The lowest value.

Mode   A calculation of an average by selecting the most common value in a list.

Modelling   Applying mark-up to text so that a text analysis program will be able to analyse it.

Moving averages   The calculation of the average for a set of data over a rolling set period of time (usually measured in years). Therefore a 5-year moving average will calculate the average in 5 year blocks.

Negatively skewed   A distribution of values where most of the values lie above the mean.

Normal distribution   Also called bell-shaped. A symmetrical distribution of values, that is, equal numbers of larger and smaller values.

Null   An entry in a database that has no value.

One-to-many relationships   Where records in one table match many in the second, but those in the second table only have one match to the first.

One-to-one relationships   Where records in one table have only one match with records in a second table.

Optical Character Recognition (OCR)   A program which translates scanned text into characters.

Order   In Powerpoint, the facility which lets you determine which of overlapping objects is at the front or at the back.

Organization Chart   A Powerpoint feature that can be used for very basic family trees.

Orphan   A standalone line which is on the page following the page which contains the rest of the paragraph. To be avoided.

Outline View   A way of viewing your document which allows you to view it by chapter headings (if you have applied Styles), and move entire sections quickly and precisely.

Pictogram   A frequency distribution represented as pictures.

Pie chart   A diagram in the form of a circle used to compare a series of data. The size of each sector, or slice, corresponds to the number of a particular value. The information may be presented as raw figures or percentages.

Point graph   Also known as a scatter graph. The plots of a number of points showing the relationship between two variables.

Positively skewed   A distribution of values where most of the values lie below the mean.

Pixels per inch (ppi)   A measure of resolution for digital images.

Presentation   In Powerpoint, the equivalent of a 'document' in Word.

Primary key   One or more fields in a database whose value or values uniquely identify each record in a table.

Program   A piece of software or set of instructions.

Prosopography   The study of biographical characteristics of a related set of individuals.

Query   A method of analysing information in a database.

Query-by-example   The process of querying a database by placing criteria in a blank form.

Range   The spread between the lowest and highest values in a list.

Record   A row in a data table.

Record linkage   The process of linking records from different tables. Nominal record linkage refers to the procedure of linking names across different sources.

Relational database   Database constructed using a relational data model.

Relational model   The modelling of data into a series of tables which are linked together.

Resolution   The measure of how much information is contained in your image.

Scanning   A simple way of turning a paper-based text or image into electronic format.

Scatter graph   Also known as a point graph. The plots of a number of points showing the relationship between two variables.

Search algorithm   The underlying program which makes a search engine work.

Search engine   A facility which indexes websites and allows you to search the index by typing keywords into a search box.

Search string   A piece of text in quotation marks. Search engines and databases will return only the words in the order and style of the text in quotation marks.

SGML   Standard Generalized Markup Language. Used, for example, by cataloguers.

Slide   In Powerpoint, the equivalent of a 'page' in Word.

Sort   An operation to order information in a database or spreadsheet.

SOUNDEX   A code for standardising surnames.

Source-oriented   Databases constructed which represent virtually every single aspect of the original source material without loss.

Spam   Unwanted or undesirable e-mail.

Spreadsheet   A piece of software made up of rows and columns to analyse data.

Spyware   Software that collects personal information from a computer without the user's knowledge or permission.

Standard deviation   The measure of dispersion of a distribution around the mean.

Structured Query Language (SQL)   A computer language containing commands allowing users to analyse databases. Most database management systems allow the use of SQL commands.

Style   In Word, a preset format for a character or paragraph which allows you to manipulate all characters or paragraphs of the same style by only changing the underlying format.

Subject directory   A website which holds links to other websites about a specific subject.

Table   A collection of fields and rows. Data in a table is represented as a two dimensional array.

Telnet   A system that allows a user to log on to a remote computer.

Template   In Word, the document (with a .dot extension) in which all your Styles and various other formatting settings for your documents are stored. The default template is normal.dot, but you can create your own and apply them to any document you like.

Thumbnail   A small, low resolution version of an image.

TIFF   A lossless image file format. Recommended for archive copies and for images which still have to be manipulated.

Time-series   A set of data which is measured over a period of time.

Trend line   A line drawn through time-series data which conveys the long-term linear trend (or direction) of the data.

Trojan or Trojan horse   A malicious programme that impersonates a benign application. Not strictly a virus as it does not replicate itself but may be as destructive as a virus.

Type Frequency   A measure of how often a word found in a collocate is used in the text throughout.

URL   Uniform Resource Locator: the name used for the address of any resource on the internet.

USB   Universal Serial Bus: a standard which defines connections between devices (for example scanners or printers) to computers.

User groups   System of distributing messages to thousands of global users who are members of particular interest groups.

Variable   In a database, the field. In statistical analysis, a characteristic that may be measured.

Variable Context   A variation on KWIC where you can determine how much context you want to have displayed.

Venn diagram   A diagram representing a set or sets and the relationships between them. The sets are drawn as circles, an area of overlap between two circles contains elements that are common to both sets.

Virus   A programme which infiltrates computers or files and replicates itself repeatedly. Some viruses damage files and computer systems, but even programs that cause no obvious damage but infiltrate machines are viruses.

Virus Hoax   Not a virus, but the deliberate or unintentional broadcasting of electronic messages warning others about a virus or other malicious software program. Some hoaxes may cause as much trouble as a real virus by causing massive amounts of unnecessary e-mail.

Webmaster   A person who creates a website and makes it available to general view. Several people may in practice be involved in creating a website, but the webmaster is always the one who deals with the interface to the outside world.

Widow   A standalone line left behind on one page when the rest of the paragraph is located on the following page. To be avoided.

Wildcard   A symbol (for example ? or *) to represent an unknown character or characters.

Word List   A list of all the words in a text, with frequency of occurrence.

World Wide Web   The library of resources available via the internet.

Worm   A parasitic computer programme that replicates but does not infect other computer program files. Worms can create copies on the same computer, or can send the copies to other computers via a network.

WYSIWYG   'What you see is what you get' – a type of program which lets you create code such as HTML mark-up through an interface which shows you not the code itself, but the end result as it will later appear on the screen.

XML   Extensible Markup Language. Can be used for database or text analysis functions.

Zip drive   A medium for the electronic storage of data.

Z-Score   A calculation of Collocate Frequency and Type Frequency which indicates whether a collocation is likely to be significant or not.

Further Reading

This guide gives a selection of some of the more important texts on each topic and has been organised as an entry into what is often interpreted as a diverse and daunting array of literature on the subject of ICT and history.

► General

Although many of these texts are now very out of date, they may still have important advice to offer on the application of computing techniques to the study of history.

- Andrews, D. and Greenhalgh, M., *Computing for Non-Scientific Applications* (Leicester, 1987).
- Benjamin, Jules R., *A Student's Guide to History*, ninth edn (Boston and New York, 2004).
- Bocchi, F. and Denley, P. (eds), *Storia & Multimedia. Atti del Settimo Congresso Internazionale* (Manchester, 1990).
- Boonstra, O., Breure, L. and Doorn, P., *Past, Present and Future of Historical Information Science* (Amsterdam, 2004) and available online from: http://www. niwi.knaw.nl/en/geschiedenis/medewerkers/peter_doorn_home_page/new_0_ copy1/toon/.
- Cameron, Sonja, *Evaluating Internet Sites for Academic Use*: http://hca.ltsn.ac.uk/ resources/Briefing_Papers/bp2.php/.
- Denley, P. and Hopkin, D. (eds), *History and Computing* (Manchester, 1987).
- Denley, P., Fogelvik, S. and Harvey, C. (eds), *History and Computing II* (Manchester, 1989).
- French, D., Hale, C., Johnson, C. and Farr, G. (eds), *Internet Based Learning: An Introduction and Framework for Higher Education and Business* (London, 1999).
- Genet, J-P. and Zampolli, A. (eds), *Computers and the Humanities* (Aldershot, 1992).
- Greenstein, D. I., *A Historian's Guide to Computing* (Oxford, 1994).
- Hall, R. and Harding, D. (eds), *Managing ICT in the Curriculum* (Middlesbrough, 2001).

- Higgs, E., *History and Electronic Artefacts* (Oxford, 1998).
- Hockney, S. (ed.), *A Guide to Computer Applications in the Humanities* (London, 1980).
- Lloyd-Jones, R. and Lewis, M. J., *Using Computers in History: A Practical Guide* (London, 1996).
- Mawdsley, E. and Munck, T., *Computers for Historians: An Introductory Guide* (Manchester, 1993).
- Mawdsley, E., Morgan, N., Richmond, L. and Trainor, R. (eds) *History and Computing III. Historians, Computers and Data. Applications in Research and Teaching* (Manchester, 1990).
- McCrank, L. J., *Historical Information Science. An Emerging Discipline* (Medford, NJ, 2002).
- Miall, D. S., *Humanities and the Computer: New Directions* (Oxford, 1990).
- Phillips, J. A. (ed.), *Computing Parliamentary History* (Edinburgh, 1994).
- Quality Assurance Agency, *History* (Gloucester, 2000) and available online from: http://www.qaa.ac.uk.
- Rahtz, S. (ed.), *A Guide to Computer Applications in the Humanities* (Chichester, 1987).
- Rhodes, Neil and Sawday, Jonathan, *The Renaissance Computer: Knowledge Technology in the First Age of Print* (London, 2000).
- Schürer, K. and Oeppen, J., 'Calculating days of the week and some related problems with using calendars of the past', *History and Computing*, 2 (1990), 107–18.
- Shorter, E., *The Historians and the Computer: A Practical Guide* (New Jersey, 1971).
- Townsend, S., Chappell, C. and Struijve, O., *A Guide to Creating Digital Resources from Historical Documents* (Oxford, 1999) and available online from: http://hds.essex.ac.uk/g2gp/digitising_history/index.asp/.
- Trickle, D. (ed.), *Writing, Teaching and Researching History in the Electronic Age* (New York, 1998).

▶ Historical databases

The introductory section gives further reading suggestions on the design and construction of historical databases using structured and unstructured texts. There is also reading on alternatives to the relational model of database design for historians. Two subsections introduce the more specialised literature on record linkage and coding issues.

- Borodkin, L. and Doorn, P. (eds), *Data Modelling, Modelling History* (Moscow, 2000).
- Bradley, J., 'Relational database design and the reconstruction of the British medical profession: constraints and strategies', *History and Computing*, 6 (1994), 71–84.

- Breure, L., 'Interactive data entry: problems, models, solutions', *History and Computing*, 7 (1995), 30–49.
- Burt, J., and Beaumont James, T., 'Source-orientated data processing. The triumph of the micro over the macro?', *History and Computing*, 8 (1996), 160–8.
- Champion, J., 'Relational databases and the Great Plague in London, 1665', *History and Computing*, 5 (1996), 2–12.
- Denley, P., 'Models, sources and users. Historical database design in the 1990s', *History and Computing*, 6 (1994), 33–44.
- Greenstein, D. I., 'A source-oriented approach to history and computing. The relational database', *Historical Social Research/Historische Sozialforschung*, 14 (1989), 9–16.
- Harvey, C., Green, E. M. and Corfield, P., *The Westminster Historical Database* (Bristol, 1998).
- Harvey, C. and Press, J., *Databases in Historical Research* (Basingstoke, 1996).
- Overton, M. A., 'Computer management system for probate inventories', *History and Computing*, 7 (1995), 135–43.
- Price, G. and Gray, A., 'Object oriented databases and their application to historical data', *History and Computing*, 6 (1994), 44–52.
- Thaller, M., *KLEIO. A Database System* (St. Katharinen, 1993).
- Weatherill, L. and Hemingway, V., *Using and Designing Databases for Academic Work. A Practical Guide* (Newcastle, 1994).
- Welling, G. M., 'A strategy for intelligent input programs for structured data', *History and Computing*, 5 (1993), 35–41.
- Woollard, M. and Denley, P. (eds), *The Sorcerers's Apprentice. KLEIO Case Studies* (St. Katharinen, 1996).

Record linkage

- Adman, P., 'Record linkage theory and practice: a matter of confidence', *History and Computing*, 9 (1997), 150–5.
- Adman, P., Baskerville, S. W. and Beedham, K. F., 'Computer-*Assisted* record linkage: or how best to optimise links without generating errors', *History and Computing*, 4 (1992), 21–5.
- Baldwin, J., Acheson, E. and Graham, W. (eds), *Textbook of Medical Record Linkage* (Oxford, 1987).
- Baskerville, S. W., ' "Preferred linkage" and the analysis of voter behaviour in eighteenth-century England', *History and Computing*, 1 (1989), 112–20.
- Davies, H. R., 'Automated record linkage of census enumerators' books and registration data. Obstacles, challenges and solutions', *History and Computing*, 4 (1992), 16–26.

- Harvey, C. and Green, E. M., 'Record linkage algorithms: efficiency, selection and relative confidence', *History and Computing*, 6 (1994), 143–52.
- Harvey, C., Green, E. M. and Corfield, P. J., 'Record linkage theory and practice. An experiment in the application of multiple pass linkage algorithms', *History and Computing*, 8 (1996), 78–90.
- King, S., 'Record linkage in a protoindustrial community', *History and Computing*, 4 (1992), 27–33.
- Wrigley, E. A. (ed.), *Identifying People in the Past* (London, 1973).

Coding and classification

- Bloothooft, G., 'Corpus-based name standardisation', *History and Computing*, 6 (1994), 39–56.
- Greenstein, D. I., 'Standard, meta-standard. A framework for coding occupational data', *Historical Social Research/Historische Sozialforschung*, 16 (1991), 3–22.
- Greenstein, D. I., *Modelling Historical Data. Towards a Standard for Encoding and Exchanging Machine-Readable Texts* (St. Katharinen, 1991).
- Morris, R. J., 'Occupational coding. Principles and examples', *Historical Social Research/Historische Sozialforschung*, 15 (1990), 3–29.
- Schürer, K. and Diederiks, H. (ed.), *The Use of Occupations in Historical Analysis* (St. Katherinen, 1993).

► Geographical information systems

Spatial analysis using the computer is becoming increasingly important to historians, particularly as the software becomes easier to use. These texts give indications of the scope and practical application of GIS to historical study.

- Gregory, I., *A Place in History. A Guide to Using GIS in Historical Research* (AHDS, 2002) and available online from: http://hds.essex.ac.uk/g2gp/gis/index.asp
- Knowles, A. K., *Past Times, Past Place. GIS for History* (Redlands, CA, 2002).
- Piotukh, N. V., 'The application of GIS techniques to Russian historical research. The Novorgev district used as a case study', *History and Computing*, 8 (1996), 169–84.

► Text Aanalysis

The references in this section give advice on marking up text for digital analysis.

- Aumann, S., Ebeling, H.-H., Fricke, H.-R. *et al.*, 'From digital archive to digital edition', *Historical Social Research/Historische Sozialforschung*, 41 (1999), 101–44.
- Robinson, P., *The Digitisation of Primary Textual Sources* (Oxford, 1993).

● Robinson, P., *The Transcription of Primary Textual Sources Using SGML* (Oxford, 1994).

▶ Quantitative methods

For further information and guidance on more complex quantitative historical methods consult the following texts:

● Darcy, R. and Rohrs, R. C., *A Guide to Quantitative History* (Westport, Ct, 1995).
● Feinstein, C. and Thomas, M., *Making History Count: A Primer in Quantitative Methods for Historians* (Cambridge, 2002).
● Floud, R., *An Introduction to Quantitative Methods for Historians*, second edn (London, 1979).
● Hudson, P., *History by Numbers: An Introduction to Quantitative Approaches* (London, 2000).
● Lee, C. H., *The Quantitative Approach to Economic History* (London, 1977).
● Wrigley, E. A. (ed.), *Nineteenth-Century Society: Essays in the Use of Quantitative Methods for the Study of Social Data* (Cambridge, 1972).

Index

Note: Page numbers in italics refer to figures and tables.